AUS
AUSTRALIA
AMAZING EXPERIENCES
DISCOVERY TOURS
PULL-OUT MAP
Travel with
Insider Tips

MARCO POLO TOP HIGHLIGHTS

BLUE MOUNTAINS NATIONAL PARK ★1

Endless forests, steep gorges and sacred Aboriginal sites: welcome to the wilderness on Sydney's doorstep.

➤ p. 54, Sydney

KAKADU NATIONAL PARK ★2

The country's tropical north offers rock paintings, crocodiles and fascinating landscapes.

➤ p. 116, Northern Territory

GREAT BARRIER REEF ★3

Off the coast of Queensland, the reef is a must for divers, sailors and nature lovers.

Tip: No pricey underwater cameras needed on Lady Elliot Island. The reef starts at the beach!

➤ p. 88, Queensland

OPERA HOUSE ★4

The shell-shaped building on Sydney Harbour is an architectural masterpiece – and a Down Under landmark.

Tip: The northern tip of the Domain (near Mrs Macquarie's Chair) offers incredible views of the Opera House.

➤ p. 45, Sydney

ULURU-KATA TJUTA NATIONAL PARK ★5

These days you can't climb it, but imposing Uluru (formerly Ayers Rock) remains a must-see.

➤ p. 121, Northern Territory

BAROSSA VALLEY ★6

Wine, rye bread and smoked ham – plus historical villages with beautiful scenery.

➤ p. 151, South Australia

KANGAROO ISLAND 7

The finest honey, delicious gin, plus penguins, koalas, huge seal colonies and, of course, kangaroos.

Tip: Follow the boardwalk at Admirals Arch to the end. Seals slumber and play-wrestle on the cliffs here.

➤ p. 150, South Australia

GREAT OCEAN ROAD 9

One of the world's most stunning coastal roads, with bizarre rock formations, impressive cliffs (photo), wonderful views and mysterious forests.

Tip: Walk down Gibson Steps near the Twelve Apostles. At low tide, you'll come face to face with the rocks.

➤ p. 174, Discovery Tours

CRADLE MOUNTAIN-LAKE ST CLAIR NATIONAL PARK 8

Immerse yourself in Tasmania's untamed landscape: rugged mountain peaks, still lakes deeper than you could imagine, swamps and moss-covered primeval forests.

➤ p. 167, Tasmania

K'GARI (FRASER ISLAND) 10

The world's largest sand island offers endless beaches, with dingoes on land and whales and dolphins offshore.

Tip: Boat tours between August and October offer the perfect opportunity to spot a humpback whale.

➤ p. 96, Queensland

CONTENTS

NORTHERN TERRITORY
QUEENSLAND
WESTERN AUSTRALIA
SOUTH AUSTRALIA
SYDNEY
NEW SOUTH WALES
VICTORIA
TASMANIA

CONTENTS

Plan your visit
$-$$$ Price categories
(*) Premium-rate phone number

Eating/drinking
Shopping
Nightlife
Top beaches

Sustainable activities
Budget activities
Family activities
Classic experiences
MARCO POLO Bucket list

(A2) Refers to removable pull-out map
(0) Located off the map

Hike the Overland Track through Cradle Mountain-Lake St Clair National Park

BEST OF AUSTRALIA

The view of Uluru at sunset is hard to beat

BEST GREEN & FAIR

SUSTAINABLE ACTIVITIES

NO CHEMICALS, PLEASE!

Lots of environmental dangers threaten the ocean: one of them is sun cream. In Australia, wearing sun cream is essential, but you can choose a brand that is less damaging to marine life. Products that contain oxybenzone and octinoxate should be avoided. Zinc oxide is less harmful. Even better, wear a full-body neoprene wetsuit instead.

EAT LIKE THE LOCALS

Of course you can find organic restaurants in Australia, but even more common are eateries that offer *bush tucker*; in other words, meals prepared using Indigenous Australian methods and local ingredients. A sustainable way to dine.

➤ p. 30, Eating & drinking

PROTECT THE CORAL

Every visitor to the Great Barrier Reef pays an environmental tax that supports coral-protection efforts. At *Passions of Paradise*, for example, marine biologists accompany tourist diving trips to document changes to the reef and replant broken corals.

➤ p. 103, Queensland

SUPPORT AUSTRALIAN ARTISTS

If you want to buy a didgeridoo, boomerang or a painting to take home with you, don't buy it from the nearest souvenir shop. Instead, source your chosen craft from an artisans' cooperative, such as *Aboriginal Fine Arts* in Darwin (photo).

➤ p. 114, Northern Territory

ISLAND HONEY

Island Beehive is a certified producer of organic honey. Its beekeepers look after more than 800 beehives on Kangaroo Island, which are carefully transported around the island so that the local flora is evenly pollinated.

➤ p. 150, South Australia

BEST
ON A BUDGET

FOR SMALLER WALLETS

FEEDING TIME

In the *Koala Hospital*, a large animal clinic run by volunteers in Port Macquarie, ailing koalas are nursed back to good health and returned to the wild. The best time to visit (for a small admission fee) is 3pm when the cuddly marsupials are fed.

➤ p. 62, New South Wales

ART FOR ART'S SAKE

Admission to Australia's biggest art gallery, the *National Gallery of Australia* in Canberra's government district, won't cost you a cent. Just be sure to allow plenty of time, because there are over 160,000 works by Australian and international artists.

➤ p. 67, New South Wales

FREE TRANSPORT

No tickets are needed for the *City Circle Tram* (photo) that travels around Melbourne's city centre. Many sights can easily be reached on foot from the tram stops.

➤ p. 76, Victoria

SWIM IN THE CITY

As the tropical town of Cairns doesn't have a decent sandy beach, a generously sized recreational oasis has been created between the pedestrian precinct and the coastal promenade with saltwater pools, a sunbathing area and barbecues. The *Esplanade Swimming Lagoon* is a popular meeting place – not least because it's free.

➤ p. 103, Queensland

ADELAIDE GREETERS

The friendly folk who welcome visitors to their city are know as the *Adelaide Greeters*. The free service is provided by volunteers and is currently offered in Sydney, Melbourne, Brisbane and Cairns, as well as Adelaide.

➤ p. 146, South Australia

BEST WITH CHILDREN

FUN FOR YOUNG & OLD

CHILD'S PLAY

Take the kids to one of Australia's many impressive playgrounds and they're sure to be talking about it for years to come. At the water-based *children's playground at Darling Harbour* (photo), for example, everyone – big and small alike – will get their money's worth. Just make sure to pack a change of clothes!

➤ p. 49, Sydney

MAKING LEARNING FUN

The *Questacon* in Canberra is full of irresistible experiments. Who hasn't dreamed of playing air hockey against a robot, experiencing a simulated earthquake or finding out what triggers a tsunami?

➤ p. 67, New South Wales

CROCODILE ALERT

On a *boat ride along the Adelaide River*, you can watch saltwater crocodiles leap gracefully out of the water for the bait that is held over the railing. An unforgettable experience!

➤ p. 114, Northern Territory

MEET THE SMILING MARSUPIALS

Quokkas are small and undeniably cute marsupials. You can see them in the wild on *Rottnest Island* off the coast of Perth.

➤ p. 130, Western Australia

UP CLOSE & PERSONAL WITH KANGAROOS

Of course, you can see kangaroos, koalas and emus in the wild in Australia, but you need a certain amount of luck and patience to do so. At the *Cleland Wildlife Park* in Adelaide, the animals live in a natural bush environment and you can even feed them.

➤ p. 148, South Australia

BEST

CLASSIC EXPERIENCES

ONLY IN AUSTRALIA

GLAMPING WITH WALLABIES & WOMBATS

Camp out in the bush at *Wilderness Retreats* in Victoria's Wilsons Promontory National Park. You'll experience all the sights and sounds of the outback from the comfort of a luxury tent.

➤ p. 87, Victoria

CREATURE COMFORTS

The *Lone Pine Koala Sanctuary* on the outskirts of Brisbane is the largest koala animal park in the world, as well as being home to other native animals. You can come face to face with platypuses, gawky flightless birds, tame kangaroos and other marsupials.

➤ p. 93, Queensland

A TASTE OF AUSTRALIA

The innovative menu served in the popular *Ochre Restaurant* in Cairns prides itself on showcasing Australian ingredients: crocodile, kangaroo or emu meat, local berries and bush tomatoes.

➤ p. 103, Queensland

EXPERIENCE LOCAL CULTURE

Cook damper (unleavened bread), dig through the mud for water caltrop (water chestnuts) and discover what ants taste like. On the *Animal Tracks Safari*, visitors spend a day exploring the far-flung corners of the *Kakadu National Park* and learning about the area's millennia-old Indigenous food traditions with a local guide.

➤ p. 116, Northern Territory

WINE TASTING ON TWO WHEELS

Many wineries offer wine tasting (photo) – sometimes even for free. On the *Riesling Trail* in the Clare Valley you can even explore the vineyards by bike – but remember: traffic and alcohol don't mix!

➤ p. 152, South Australia

GET TO KNOW AUSTRALIA

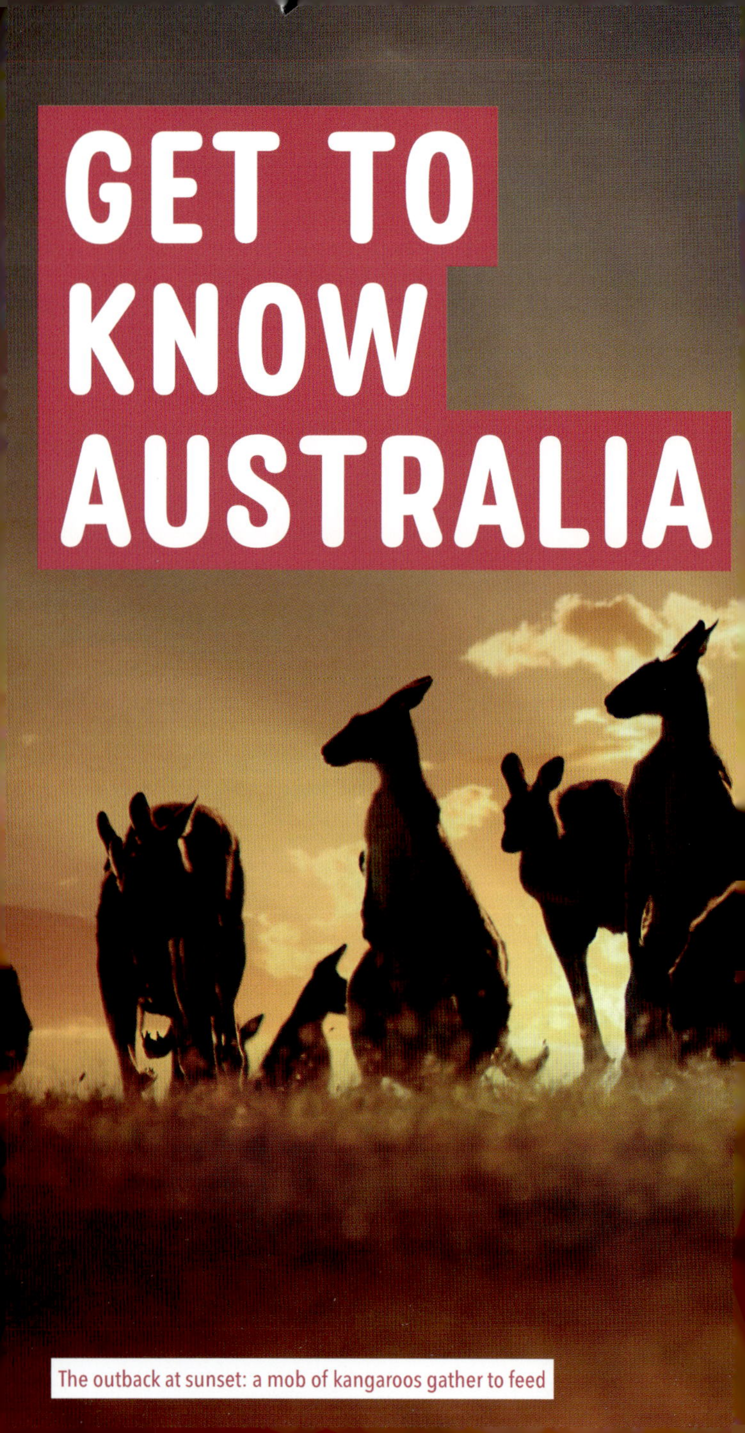

The outback at sunset: a mob of kangaroos gather to feed

DISCOVER AUSTRALIA

The sweeping lines of Elizabeth Quay Bridge join Perth City to the waterfront

Everyone is familiar with Sydney Opera House, Uluru (Ayers Rock), boomerangs and kangaroos. And everyone knows that the spiders are poisonous, that koalas sleep a lot and that Australians are pretty laid-back. But, let's be honest, many visitors from the Northern Hemisphere don't know a whole lot more about the vast red continent on the other side of the planet.

THE UNKNOWN SOUTH

In historical terms, it's not that long since people in Europe first became aware of Australia. Until Captain James Cook's return from his first South Sea voyage in 1771, existence of the "Terra Australis Incognita" – the unknown land in the south – was just a suspicion. Imagine it: the machine age had begun in Europe, and

70,000–64,000 BCE Aboriginal people settle Australia

1770 Captain James Cook claims the continent for the British Crown

1788 Great Britain uses Australia as a penal colony

1851 Gold is discovered, drawing people from across the globe

1901 The colonies unite to form a federation

1905–1970 Aboriginal Australian children are taken from their families – history's stolen generation

astronomers knew how to calculate the exact distance between the Sun and the Earth, but somehow we had completely overlooked the existence of an entire continent, an earth mass only slightly smaller than the size of Europe.

And what a bizarre world it was: the trees shed their bark instead of their leaves; swans were black, not white; the seasons were the wrong way round. And the naturalists could not find any words for the newly discovered creatures, let alone allocate them to any of the existing categories. "It is not possible to compare it to a European animal because it does not bear the slightest resemblance to any I know," was how Joseph Banks, a man not otherwise known to be lost for words, tried to describe a kangaroo. Little wonder, then, that these brief descriptions captured the imagination and created such a stir. It was to be many, many years before naturalists began to fill in the gaps in their knowledge. The fascination remains to this day.

LAND OF THE DREAMTIME

Although Europeans still consider Australia to be a young country, to Aboriginal Australians it is anything but. Australia's First Peoples had inhabited the continent for at least 60,000 years by the time Captain Cook set anchor here. This makes Australian Aboriginal culture the oldest continuously existing culture in human history. But that's not all: Aboriginal beliefs, ways of life and spirituality are so enduring that, even today, Indigenous Australians are able to interpret

1942 Japanese bombers attack Darwin. Australian soldiers fight for the Allies

1999 Republic referendum: Australia chooses to retain the British monarch as its head of state

2008 Prime Minister Kevin Rudd issues an apology to the victims of the stolen generation

2019/2020 "Black Summer": a season of devastating bush fires

2025 The social democratic Labour Party under Prime Minister Anthony Albanese wins the parliamentary elections the messages handed down by their ancestors in their rock paintings or verses with the same ease as they would, perhaps, an SMS from a modern-day cousin. A deep affinity with their land has resulted in a lifestyle that has stood in a perfect balance with nature for thousands of years.

In Aboriginal Australian mythology, every single person is a direct descendant of an ancestral being featured in the Aboriginal creation story. Representations of this era, called the Dreamtime, are handed down in paintings and songs. However, a person is only initiated into the knowledge to which they are entitled on the basis of their gender, age and ranking. Uninitiated outsiders are only given brief insights into a very small part of Indigenous Australian mythology.

TWO WORLDS COLLIDE

The Aboriginal peoples of Australia see it as their role to look after the land and all living beings on it, and to preserve the natural balance. The idea of ownership, of possession, brought in by the white settlers was as strange to Australia's Indigenous populations as farming or the building of permanent settlements. Whites, in turn, made a fatal assumption when they saw the lack of solid buildings and the absence of any obvious cultivation of the land: in the Proclamation of Terra Nullius, they declared Australia to be a no man's land. The subsequent seizure of land caused the destruction of natural habitats and sparked brutal confrontations between the Indigenous people and the new arrivals. The diseases the settlers brought with them did even more harm. In many areas, local Indigenous populations were virtually wiped out within a very short time. The fiction of Terra Nullius was not repealed until 1992, and coexistence of Aboriginal and settler cultures remains a contentious and emotive topic in Australia to this day, with many open wounds.

DIFFERENT COUNTRIES, DIFFERENT YARDSTICKS

By land, it's about 4,000km from Sydney on the east coast to Perth in the west. Travel from Adelaide in the south to Darwin in the tropical north, and you'll find yourself clocking up at least 3,000km. The continent's almost 7.7 million km² is home to just under 28 million people. These are the sort of benchmark figures you need to keep in mind when planning your trip.

So what appeals to you about Australia? Is it the charm of the cosmopolitan centres such as Sydney and Melbourne? Or the endless deserted sandy beaches or the Great Barrier Reef? Are you looking for the perfect wave? Or are you drawn to the world of the outback? Whichever destinations you choose, leave time and space for spontaneous exploration, for surprising encounters and for sunsets that are still fascinating long after the glowing sphere has disappeared beyond the horizon. Because these are the experiences that you will never forget.

INSIDER TIP
Spontaneity and sunsets

AT A GLANCE

27,800,000
inhabitants

Sydney: 5,560,000
London: 9,840,000

35,877km

Coastline

Longest beach:
Ninety Mile Beach

151km

In the UK:
Chesil Beach: 29km

7,692,000km²
Area

Sydney: 12,368km²
UK: 243,610km²

LONGEST STRAIGHT RAILWAY LINE IN THE WORLD

478km

through the Nullarbor Plain

POPULATION BORN OUTSIDE AUSTRALIA

30.7%

MOST POPULAR TIMES TO VISIT SYDNEY

September–November
and
March–May

20 UNESCO WORLD HERITAGE SITES

including the Great Barrier Reef, Daintree Rainforest, K'gari (Fraser Island), Sydney Opera House

MOUNT KOSCIUSZKO

is the tallest mountain at 2,228m

Ben Nevis: 1,344m

DAYS OF SUNSHINE IN SYDNEY

107
per year

UNDERSTAND AUSTRALIA

BULADJANG, OR THE REVENGE OF URANIUM

In the tropical north of Australia is a region that has been taboo to the local Aboriginal people for thousands of years. *Buladjang* – which means "Sickness Country" – is what they call this mystical region close to Kakadu National Park. According to the traditional Aboriginal story of creation, this is where the ancestral Bula spirit created the landscape as he walked and hunted: marshes, savannah woodlands and rocks. When he had finished his work, Bula went underground to rest, and must not be disturbed as he can cause all kinds of natural disasters.

The Aboriginal people have known for thousands of years that the water here is toxic, and that eating anything that grows here causes disease. The white prospectors who burst on the scene at the beginning of the 20th century and called the saltwater crocodiles "alligators" and described the local people as "primitive", thought this was all most suspicious. Without wasting too much time on international basic principles or niceties such as respect, they forced their way into the forbidden zone – and found the richest uranium ore deposits on the planet.

You might now ask yourself what this story has to do with Australia today. It's easy: it is a typical, often-repeated example of the crass clash between two world views that could not be more different from each other, and whose collateral damage continues to the present.

It is possibly one of the most unfortunate ironies in the history of mankind that an ancient people, who have always strived to leave only the faintest traces on Mother Earth, even after thousands of years, should be the custodian of a mineral that not only gave rise to a new industrial revolution in the Western world, but also led to the development of various devastating weapons of mass destruction. The interaction between Indigenous and incoming people and the coexistence of their cultures remain extremely sensitive issues to this day.

GREY (& OTHER) NOMADS

The Aussies love camping. It's a tradition: even the pioneers moved around the country with a *swag*, which is something inbetween a tent and a sleeping bag. To this day, Australians like to pack up all their gear at the weekend and build a temporary home out of canvas and tent poles somewhere in the wilderness. During school holidays, expect to compete with hordes of Australian families for space on the campsite. Oh, and then, of course, there are the "grey nomads", for whom camping is both a leisure activity and a philosophy of life. These are pensioners who love travelling, and often swap their homes for a caravan or mobile home to travel the

Get used to sharing your campsite with the local wildlife

continent in tune with the seasons. By the way, these mature globe-trotters are an inexhaustible source of insider tips for travellers.

CREEPY CRAWLIES

Of all the strange creatures in the Australian animal world, ranging from cute to scary, visitors probably pay the most attention to its spiders. Just how dangerous are they? In fact, there are a number of spiders whose poison can be fatal for humans. They include Sydney's funnel-web spider and the harmless-looking redback spider, which is found all over Australia. The good news is that, with the introduction of antidotes in the early 1980s, the number of deaths from spider bites dropped to zero. However, it is important that you seek medical assistance promptly if you are bitten. Be particularly careful on walkabouts in the bush. Walking face-first into a vast, thickly spun spider's web is about as creepy as suddenly having a parachute thrown over you – just slightly less pleasant.

DON'T ADAPT TOO MUCH!

Almost half of all Australians either emigrated here themselves or had at least one parent who did. But multiculturalism, far from being just hype in Australia, is the government's official creed. Immigrants are encouraged to preserve their cultural and linguistic singularities, because they are the core of the national identity. New arrivals never have a strange culture forced upon them, but are asked what they bring with them that will enrich

The fantastical duck-billed platypus puzzled naturalists for decades

Australia. Can this work? Decide for yourself in multicultural Melbourne.

By 2050, the population of Australia is predicted to have risen from around 27 million today to 50 million, largely as a result of immigration. That said, the authorities remain very selective about which immigrants are allowed in, and the criteria are continually being made stricter. Immigration slowed dramatically during the Covid-19 pandemic; both population growth and economic growth were very limited during this period.

BEASTLY FUN

Furry beasts that spend the day sleeping in the branches of trees. Marsupials that leap across the ground as if on springs. Coin-sized insects with a poisonous bite that can fell a horse. The Creator must have been in a funny mood when he focused his attention on Australia's animal world. Can you imagine what the early settlers must have thought of all this?

Here is just one example: the *platypus* posed quite a conundrum for the first naturalists. In fact, those who had never seen one in the wild thought the specimen that was sent back to England was so odd that it could only be a fake – a joke by a clever taxidermist. It rather resembled a flattened beaver with a duck's bill. However, its reproductive habits were even more curious than its external appearance. Ninety years passed before a Scottish biologist finally managed to slay an unfortunate female with an unlaid egg in her womb. This was the first evidence of the existence of an egg-laying mammal – also referred to as a monotreme. Once again, Australia had turned the organised world of the Europeans upside down.

Today, climate change is taking its toll on Australian wildlife. The Bramble Cay mosaic-tailed rat, found solely on the small island of the same name just north of the Great Barrier Reef, went down in history as the first mammal to be driven to extinction by climate change.

GREEN MOVEMENTS ON THE RED CONTINENT

When it comes to environmentalism, the contrasts in Australia are at least as marked as in the environment itself. The first settlers demonstrated little restraint in the way they used and treated nature. It's not hard to see why: most of them were convicts who had been sent here against their will. Their only aim was to create a tolerable existence for themselves in this unforgiving landscape. But the trees continued to fall long after the initial need to fell them for survival passed. Diggers continue their search for profitable mineral resources to this day, even in protected areas. This is something even the first environmental activists, who organised themselves politically here before any other country in the world, were unable to change.

Australia feels the full force of the consequences of climate change: cyclones and storms regularly devastate and flood regions in the north and east of the continent, for example during the first three-year La Niña weather phenomenon (2020–2023), when entire towns were inundated.

TRUE OR FALSE?

IT'S ALL DUST & DESERT

OK, granted, the numbers do little to disprove the old cliché: 70 per cent of the Australian continent is either arid or semi-arid – in other words, it's dry. But Australians tend to settle somewhere else entirely, with over 80 per cent of the population living less than 100km from the coast. For the most part, urban Australia is as modern, futuristic even, as Manhattan or Dubai. So if you're dreaming of an adventure that's a little more *Crocodile Dundee*, you'll need to head for the outback.

AUSSIES LOVE A FOSTER'S

Well, maybe a few … on holiday in Europe, where the largest-selling Australian beer brand makes the most of its "down under" connotations, despite it now being brewed across the globe. But at home Australians prefer a glass (or two) of Carlton Draught, Castlemaine XXXX or Victoria Bitter. Australians are also increasingly enjoying craft beers from the many microbreweries scattered across the country. Why not try a Balter XPA, Fat Yak or 4 Pines when you get the chance?

Added to this are the danger of bush fires during the long, hot dry periods and mass coral bleaching events on the Great Barrier Reef, which have occurred ever more frequently in the last few decades

TYPICAL AUSSIE

One nice characteristic from the pioneering era has managed to survive to this day – the seemingly boundless helpfulness of the Australians, regardless of whether you have a puncture in the outback or have lost your way in Sydney or Melbourne. Appointments are rescheduled just to get you back on the road, maps are organised, routes explained – and all with a patience and friendliness that make most Europeans gasp in amazement. At such moments you really experience how strong the bond between Australians actually is, and that the solidarity they feel for one another is one of the nation's fundamental values.

Australians react very sensitively to arrogance and presumptuousness. They resent it when celebrities or politicians seem too entitled or distant (or even, some allege, too successful). It's a common feeling that these people need to be brought down to earth. Like the British, they call this "tall poppy syndrome"". Poppies that get too tall, many think, need to be cut down to size.

GOD SAVE THE KING

The British monarch, King Charles III, is Australia's head of state. Charles appoints a governor general as his representative, as suggested by the Australian government. And this representative in turn gives his or her blessing to the ministers who are suggested by the prime minister. Do you think all that's rather complicated and outdated? A referendum in 1999 surprisingly confirmed that Australians would rather remain loyal to the Crown than become a republic. Nonetheless, republican noises are still made from time to time, and it is not beyond the realms of possibility that Australia may question its position as a federal parliamentary constitutional monarchy before much longer with another referendum.

THE RACE THAT STOPS THE NATION

If you happen to be travelling unsuspectingly on a bus in Australia at just before 3pm on the first Tuesday in November, don't be surprised if the driver suddenly pulls over, slams on the brake and without further ado disappears into the pub on the corner of the street; or if you're in the supermarket, you may find that the checkout remains unmanned for several minutes. The street may suddenly completely empty – where is everybody? It's Melbourne Cup Day! And there's a good reason why Australia's most prestigious horse race is known as "the race that stops the nation".

No other day in the year unites the Australian nation like this one: the day on which the country stops – to collectively watch the horse they've backed. About 80 per cent of the adult Australian population put their money on at least one horse, which means the Cup has long since grown beyond the domain of true racing fans. It's just part of the charm of this event that many an ambitious speculator who has spent months studying the form and performance of the horses ends up shredding their betting slips in sheer frustration, while the slightly tipsy lady standing close by is amused by the fact that she only chose the one that went on to win because she could still say its name after consuming countless cocktails. Melbourne Cup Day is even an official public holiday in the state of Victoria.

FLYING DOCTORS

The first medical emergency service by air in the world began in 1928 as the Australian Aerial Medical Service in the small town of Cloncurry in Queensland, after the Presbyterian pastor John Flynn had seen the misery of those living in the outback for himself. Being so far from medical help, many people died as the result of injuries and illnesses that would have been treated easily in towns. Today, the Royal Flying Doctor Service (RFDS) operates from bases across the country, from which they serve an area of 7.3 million km², roughly 30 times the size of the United Kingdom.

The Flying Doctors deal with medical cases – from births to accidents – in the outback

EATING SHOPPING SPORT

Melbourne has a diverse and dynamic restaurant scene

TEEN

EATING & DRINKING

Try barramundi cooked in paperbark, Moroccan-spiced kangaroo tenderloin or pizza topped with crocodile meat, and add to that a craft beer or glass of Sauvignon Blanc from the local winery. Australia is a paradise for lovers of fresh, light and varied food.

ONCE A GOURMET DESERT …

Back in the late 1990s, Australia's culinary culture still left a bad taste (sometimes literally) in the mouth of the country's gourmets. The restaurant on the corner offered the same overcooked steak and limp vegetables as the pub across the street. Bread came in a plastic bag, and it didn't take much to leave it compacted to just an inch or so thick. Beer was only available from industrial breweries that seemed to value quantity over quality.

… NOW A CULINARY MELTING POT

Thankfully, that's a thing of the past. Actually, it's better than that. Today, Australia offers a wealth of culinary experiences that even a local would struggle to get through.

Australia has the many immigrants from across the globe to thank for that. Over the past few decades, they have made the country their home, responding to the poor food on offer with a mix of homesickness and inspiration. First, whole neighbourhoods sprung up devoted entirely to Italian or Chinese cuisine, for example. New cuisines quickly joined the pot, and now you can find *yum cha* next to fish and chips, while further down the street fresh falafels are frying and Vietnamese *pho* is bubbling away.

Grilled red mullet with coleslaw (left); pavlova (right)

FUSION FOOD

INSIDER TIP
Multicultural menus
Today you'll find specialities from Spain to Shanghai and Siberia to Samoa not just on the same street, but also often on the same plate.

How about, for example, pork belly with oyster sauce? French scallops with Vietnamese coleslaw? Welcome to fusion food, the trend that brings together the most diverse culinary cultures and arts in a single dish. And there's nowhere better to sample the success of these blends than Melbourne or Sydney.

MARKET DAY

No trip is complete without a visit to one of the old markets, such as Central Market in Adelaide or the Queen Victoria Market in Melbourne. You'll find a stunning variety of fresh salads, exotic vegetables and tasty fruit. And most of it is grown in Australia – juicy fragrant mangos, sweet pineapples, bananas and coconuts from the tropical north; aromatic peaches, passionfruit, melons, lychees and citrus fruit from Victoria and New South Wales; and apples and pears from Tasmania. On top of this, there are numerous Asian leafy vegetables, plus tenderstem broccoli, avocados, sweet potatoes and a huge selection of fresh herbs and spices.

Meat comes from cattle and sheep raised naturally on open pastureland and from kangaroos, emus and crocodiles. The large fish markets stock everything the ocean, rivers and lakes have to offer, such as tender white barramundi from the saltwaters of the north, John Dory from the bottom of the ocean, excellent fresh tuna, tangerine-coloured salmon, and delicious giant crabs, oysters and other shellfish.

Wine from the Margaret River region is highly regarded by connoisseurs

ABORIGINAL FOOD

Bush tucker – food made from local ingredients that are prepared using Indigenous Australian cooking methods – has long since made it onto the country's restaurant menus, and is even the calling card for many fine-dining establishments. At *Restaurant Botanic*, for example, in Adelaide's botanic garden, you can try crocodile tongue, juniper-smoked kangaroo or emu fillet with quandong fruits. Or spoil yourself with a meal under the stars at the prize-winning *Tali Wiru*, with a view of Uluru. Join a foraging tour with an Aboriginal or Torres Strait Islander guide to gain insights into the bush larder.

CRAFT BEER & FINE WINE

A pint of draught beer from one of the big breweries might lack something of the taste and zest of European beers. However, the same cannot be said about the often excellent beer produced by the various small craft breweries.

Australian wines are excellent: earthy dry reds and refreshing whites – these are world class. German and Italian immigrants took the first proper vines with them to Australia and, today, Australian wine is exported around the globe.

COFFEE AT ITS BEST

Aussies love a good cup of coffee, especially in the big cities. They developed a taste for it thanks to Italian immigrants who, from the early days, started importing their highly polished espresso machines from home. In time, Aussies developed a coffee culture of their very own. If you order a short black, you'll get a plain espresso; a long black is two-thirds water and one-third espresso. Extremely popular – and something of an invention from Australia/New Zealand – is the flat white: two shots of espresso topped up with steamed milk and finished with a layer of microfoam, not to be confused with a latte (milky coffee) or a cappuccino.

TODAY'S SPECIALS

Starters

BARBECUED PRAWNS
Marinated barbecued giant prawns

CRAB SALAD
Cooked crab on a bed of salad leaves

GARLIC BREAD
Fresh sourdough with garlic butter

Mains

BARRAMUNDI FILLETS WITH MACADAMIA NUTS
Breaded barramundi with chopped macadamia nuts, served with salad

KANGAROO BURGER WITH BEETROOT
Kangaroo patty in a burger bun with beetroot

LEG OF LAMB WITH ROASTED VEGGIES
Oven-roasted leg of lamb seasoned with garlic, rosemary and honey, served with vegetables

CROCODILE PIZZA
With optional added kangaroo or emu meat

Desserts

PAVLOVA
Meringue with fresh cream, berries, peaches, kiwis and passion fruit

LAMINGTON
Soft sponge cake dipped in chocolate and sprinkled with coconut flakes

ANZAC BISCUIT
Oat biscuit with sugar beet syrup

TIM TAM
Australia's favourite chocolate biscuit

Drinks

CRAFT BEER
Beer from an independent brewery

SAUVIGNON BLANC
From the Hunter Valley

SHIRAZ
From the Barossa Valley

FLAT WHITE
Espresso with hot milk

SHOPPING

DREAMTIME SOUVENIRS

You don't have to go far in Australian cities or tourist hotspots to find boomerangs, clap sticks or didgeridoos. Everywhere you look, there are souvenir shops selling Aboriginal handicrafts. But watch out: all too often, these are mass-produced articles that no Aboriginal Australian ever had anything to do with. But as a lay person, how can you tell the difference between genuinely hand-made crafts and copies?

INSIDER TIP
How to avoid fakes

You can rely on certified Aboriginal art galleries, cultural centres and community art centres. And check the label of authenticity, as it should have a registration number indicating the artist who made the item. Small workshops in the outback often offer the most authentic souvenirs.

PRECIOUS STONES & PEARLS

Near Broome in the north of Western Australia, elegant, cultured pearls are farmed in the coastal waters, while valuable sapphires and opals are dug from the earth in the interior of the continent. The best prices are to be obtained locally, e.g. opals in Coober Pedy (South Australia) and Lightning Ridge (New South Wales), and sapphires in the Central Highlands (Queensland). The jewellery shops in the major cities work against this by offering fancy settings. Alternatively, you could buy an uncut stone or a pearl without a setting and have your gem fashionably set by a local goldsmith back home.

OUTDOOR CLOTHING

There's an old Nordic saying: there's no such thing as bad weather, just bad clothing. *Akubra* hats (the word means

Didgeridoos and all-weather hats make great souvenirs

"head cover") are designed to cope with all kinds of weather. *Akubra* is a long-standing Australian brand that produces wide-brimmed, felt hats made from the finest rabbit fur felt. The hats protect the wearer from the scorching sun as well as downpours and sandstorms, and should really be bought at the start of your trip. Akubras can be found in all sorts of shapes in hat shops or outdoor outfitters such as R.M. Williams or Kathmandu. Quality Akubras – and only these can deal with the extremes of the Australian weather – come at a price. The same is true of Driza-Bones, the waxed coats in which stockmen in the outback face the elements, or indeed leather ankle boots that protect your feet over impassable terrain. But just as a warning, those last two might well send the weight of your suitcase skyrocketing!

"BRING BACK SOME TIM TAMS"

Your friends and colleagues might ask this of you before you set off on your trip to Australia. The thick, chocolate-covered biscuits are cheap and cheerful and practically everyone likes them.

It's a different story with Vegemite, the salty, bitter spread that is Australia's version of Marmite.

SURF'S UP

Feeling the pull of the waves? Pick pretty much any coastline suitable for surfing and you'll find surf shops and schools that not only offer courses, but also rent and sell all the right gear (boards and wetsuits). The most popular manufacturers include Quiksilver, Billabong and Hurley. For reasonably priced boards and clothing, try Anaconda outdoor shops, for example.

SPORT & ACTIVITIES

On the Australian continent, sport is more a way of life than a hobby. And when you can practise sport in the country's huge natural playgrounds, then the possibilities are endless. You can swim, surf, sail and dive in many places around the virtually infinite coastline, and in the mountains you can go climbing and even skiing. The many national parks offer endless hikes, from a short stroll to multi-day tours. Even extreme-sports enthusiasts are sure to get their money's worth.

CANOEING & KAYAKING

Australia's coastline and the rivers of Tasmania or the Snowy Mountains are ideal for sea kayaking, canoeing and rafting. There are many businesses in the hundreds of coastal resorts or on the edge of national parks that have canoes, kayaks and equipment for hire or which organise guided tours. *World Expeditions (worldexpeditions.com.au)* offer tours lasting anything from one day to two weeks *(approx. A$3,300 for six days)* all over Australia, often taking in visits to Aboriginal communities.

DIVING

Apart from the Barrier Reef *(diving qld.org.au)*, a household name in itself, there are plenty of other interesting diving areas. Ningaloo Reef in Western Australia is fantastic and far less crowded. Trial courses are a good way to familiarise yourself with this sport. A five-day basic course on the Great Barrier Reef costs around A$1,290 and is offered, for example, by *Pro Dive Cairns (tel. 07 40 31 52 55 | prodivecairns.com)*. Further information is available from *PADI (Professional Association of Diving Instructors | padi.com)*

Riding the waves at Surfer's Paradise

HIKING

The national parks are full of fabulous walking trails. Maps are available from the local tourist information centres. Some bushwalks require you to sign out at the local ranger's office before you set off, and leave information on your planned route and expected date of return with them.

Well known bushwalks include the *Coast Track* through the Royal National Park (two days) near Sydney, the *K'gari (Fraser Island) Great Walk* (six to eight days) in Queensland, and the *Overland Track* (six days) and *Three Capes Track* (four days) in Tasmania. South Australia offers the *Kangaroo Island Wilderness Trail* (five days) and walks through the Flinders Ranges, while the *Cape to Cape Track* (five to seven days) near Margaret River and the *Coastal Trail* in Cape Le Grand National Park (one to two days) are a good choice in Western Australia.

Australia's hiking trails are extremely well signposted and hard to miss. That said, hikers still get lost in the wilderness from time to time. Given the vast areas and sometimes extreme weather involved, this can end very badly, and those with little hiking experience should definitely join a guided tour *(worldexpeditions.com.au)*. General information: *auswalk.com.au, bushwalkingaustralia.org, greatwalksofaustralia.com.au.*

HORSE RIDING

You can ride all over the place in Australia: in parks, on cattle or sheep stations (hacks often being part of a stay-on-a-farm package), on beaches and through rainforests. But the horse-rider's paradise is the Snowy Mountains; try *Snowy Wilderness Boundless Adventure (1-day tour with lunch A$426 | tel. 02 64 57 23 17 | snowywilderness.com.au).*

KITESURFING

With its seemingly endless miles of deserted beaches, Australia is a paradise for kitesurfers, with a choice of spots ranging from sheltered to actively windswept, depending on your experience and appetite for risk. Kiter hotspots include the bays and beaches of Noosaville (Gold Coast), St Kilda and Brighton (Melbourne), Port Douglas (north of Cairns) and Yallingup (south of Perth). For more information, go to *surfertoday.com*.

MOUNTAIN BIKING

Although the options for conventional cycle tours on the continent are limited – not least because of the distances – there are many areas that offer the ideal terrain for mountain bikers. There is even a 14km prepared trail on South Molle in the Whitsunday Islands. In the Blue Mountains, the hilly 120km route from Glenbrook to Wentworth is quite a challenge. Twenty routes are outlined by *cycle trailsaustralia.com*, while the magazine *Australian Mountain Bike* contains plenty of interesting information *(ambmag.com.au)*. There are numerous guided tours, while *Outback Cycling (tel. 08 89 52 39 33 | outbackcycling.com)* rents bikes at Uluru (including shuttle bus from Ayers Rock Resort) and offers tours from Alice Springs to the MacDonnell Ranges.

SAILING

There are sailing schools and associations in all large Australian towns on the coast and in many resorts where

you can learn to sail or, for those with more experience, sail as a member of the crew. You can get information and price lists at local visitor information offices.

Sailing in Sydney Harbour is fun even for those who are not experienced. *Sail Australia (Cremorne | Sydney | prices on request | tel. 04 18 76 89 06 | sailaustralia.com.au)* organises sailing charters. Another great sailing area is the Whitsunday Islands; one renowned organiser of trips from Airlie Beach is *Pro Sail (tel. 07 04 55 797 33 66 | prosail.com.au)*, which offers two days from A$670.

STAND-UP PADDLEBOARDING

Whether on calm lakes or the waves of the Pacific, stand-up paddling is one

Get up close and personal with a green sea turtle on the Great Barrier Reef

of the most popular water-sports in the country. Many places offer boards and paddles for hire, so visitors can also try their luck on the water. Those with little experience should start out on calm waters. *Jervis Bay Stand Up Paddle (tel. 04 03 35 47 16 | jervis baystanduppaddle.com.au)* rents SUPs (A$50/2 hrs) and offers tours on request.

SURFING

There are surf schools on most of the monitored beaches in Australia. *Let's Go Surfing (tel. 02 93 65 18 00 | letsgosurfing.com.au)* on the beach at Maroubra organises excellent introductory courses for A$95 for two hours, including surfboard and wetsuit. Surf & stay is offered by *Mojo Surf (tel. 02 66 39 51 00 | mojosurf.com)* on the east coast in Byron Bay: five days including accommodation, breakfast, equipment and lessons for A$690.

INSIDER TIP
First surf lessons

Surfies meet up on the beaches of the Great Ocean Road, preferably Bells Beach, the Gold Coast or at the southern end of the west coast, where the waves are notoriously strong and therefore only for experienced surfers.

By contrast, the waters around Perth are perfect for beginners, while Moana Beach in southern Adelaide is also an ideal place to learn to surf, for example with *Surf & Sun (surfand sun.com.au)*. Find out more about the top spots at *surfing-waves.com* and *surfingaustralia.com*.

REGIONAL OVERVIEW

PAPUA NEW GUINEA
Arafura Sea
QUEENSLAND p. 88
Dive the reef and feast on seafood
Go for a walk with a local guide
Cairns
Coral Sea
Marvel at the reef
Great Barrier Reef
Finders R.
Diamantina R.
K'gari (Fraser Island)
Brisbane
Gold Coast
Learn to surf in paradise
NEW SOUTH WALES p. 56
Learn to surf and search for opals – it's all here!
Climb to the top
Taste wine that's as old as you are
Blue Mountains National Park
Sydney
Opera House
Barossa Valley
SYDNEY p. 40
CANBERRA
Adelaide
From harbour views to surf beaches – a global urban showstopper
Murray R.
Kangaroo Island
Melbourne
VICTORIA p. 72
Urban culture and the Great Ocean Road
Great Ocean Road
Tasman Sea
Cradle Mountain-Lake St Clair National Park
TASMANIA p. 156
Hike to the end of the world
Hobart
Delicious wine and dense rainforest go hand in hand

SYDNEY

BAREFACED BEAUTY

Few cities can offer a welcome to rival that of Sydney. After an interminable flight, you step off the train or airport shuttle at Circular Quay, and there it all is, right in front of your eyes: the buzzing harbour, the striking Opera House and the Harbour Bridge, nicknamed "the coat hanger" by the locals. Welcome to Sydney!

Australia's busiest metropolis stretches around the natural harbour like an oversized patchwork quilt, covering an area more than

Sydney's skyline is impressive by day and breathtaking by night

twice the size of Greater London. And there's no need to worry about getting bored: you could happily spend months here discovering the countless pretty beach suburbs, exploring museums, browsing the markets, admiring sumptuous mansions or sampling your way through the city's many gastronomic delights.

But who has that much time? Focus on what you know you want to see, and make sure you take time to simply soak up the atmosphere of this cosmopolitan showstopper of a city.

MARCO POLO BUCKET LIST

1 Climb to the top

Conquer your fear of heights to climb the arch of *Sydney Harbour Bridge*

➤ p. 46

The best way to reach Manly is aboard the beige and green ferry from Circular Quay. It departs every 10–20 minutes and costs around A$9.

MARCO POLO HIGHLIGHTS

★ **CIRCULAR QUAY**
Just round the corner from the Opera House, this is the beating heart of the city ➤ p. 44

★ **OPERA HOUSE**
The crown jewel in the urban showstopper that is Sydney ➤ p. 45

★ **ROYAL BOTANIC GARDENS**
Caution: loud noises! Especially when the bats wake up at dusk ➤ p. 45

★ **HARBOUR BRIDGE**
Steel steps and ladders let you explore this Sydney landmark ➤ p. 46

★ **THE ROCKS**
Historical pubs, lively restaurants and great shops ➤ p. 46

★ **DARLING HARBOUR**
Spend an evening in Sydney's liveliest harbour ➤ p. 48

★ **BLUE MOUNTAINS NATIONAL PARK**
The wilderness on Sydney's doorstep ➤ p. 54

The open-top double-decker bus operated by Big Bus Sydney passes all of Sydney's most famous sights en route to Bondi Beach. Boat trips with Captain Cook Cruises are included in the ticket price.

Discover the beauty of Sydney on foot: the 6km Bondi to Coogee Coastal Walk starts at Bondi's Iceberg Pool and includes countless "Wow!" moments.

The view of the Harbour Bridge and the Opera House is particularly beautiful at sunset

The setting could hardly be more fabulous: in the natural harbour of Port Jackson, aka Sydney Harbour, the blue ocean meets the red continent. Along its shore lies a cosmopolitan metropolis of elegant esplanades, idyllic beaches, surf breaks and dramatic coastal cliffs.

WHERE TO START?

The best starting point is **Circular Quay** at **Sydney Cove**, where the station and bus terminal are, and where the city ferries sail from. You're at the very heart of things here, with the Opera House in front of you and Harbour Bridge behind you. All the ferries and City Rail trains stop here. Driving in the city centre is not recommended.

Sydney is Australia's oldest and largest city, boasting a fascinating arts and culture scene, superb cuisine and vibrant markets. For lovers of flora and fauna, there's Australia's oldest botanical garden, whales and dolphins off the coast, and a zoo with a view of the Opera House – for giraffes and visitors alike. As you can probably guess, Sydney deserves some time. The main attractions can be reached on the Big Bus Sydney *(bigbustours.com)*.

SIGHTSEEING

1 CIRCULAR QUAY ★

Circular Quay is the main tourist artery of this thriving metropolis. Every day

millions of people set off from here to every single corner of Sydney. It's best to travel here by ferry because the views of the Opera House and Harbour Bridge from the water are sensational. If you want something a little more active, then enjoy *Sydney Harbour* from a kayak.

INSIDER TIP
Paddle across the harbour

Try a guided kayak tour in a small group with *Sydney Harbour Kayaks (rentals from A$30/hr | sydneyharbourkayaks.com.au)*. Harbour trips are offered by *Captain Cook Cruises (daily 9.30am–8pm | from A$32, whale watching May–Nov A$96 | captaincook.com.au)*.

2 OPERA HOUSE ★

The glistening shell-like roof of the Opera House, located right on the harbour, has become Sydney's landmark. The Danish architect Jørn Utzon won an architectural prize with his revolutionary design – and the right to build the Opera House in Sydney. After seven years of battling with Australian bureaucrats who said the project was too expensive, Utzon gave up. His work was only completed after a 14-year building period – and with help from the lottery that provided the necessary funding. Apparently Utzon never got to see the finished building.

The opera stage, the concert hall and a smaller theatre are housed in the Opera House. The *Architectural Tour (A$60)* gives an insight into this ambitious project that reinvented Australia's image. *Other guided tours take place daily 9am–5pm | A$45 | Bennelong Point | sydneyoperahouse.com | bus/City Rail/ferry Circular Quay, on foot along Circular Quay East | ⏲ 1–3 hrs*

3 ROYAL BOTANIC GARDENS ★

The botanical gardens in Sydney are on the harbour's most beautiful bay, not far from the Opera House. This was where the fields of the first farm in the penal colony were established. The original section of the gardens, with Australian trees and plants, was laid out in 1816.

A well-maintained path leads from the Opera House along the waterside to *Mrs Macquarie's Chair*, a seat hewn out of the rock which offers an impressive view of the Opera House and

Harbour Bridge. Governor Macquarie's wife suffered badly from homesickness and used to sit here watching the ships arriving from her home country. The cool grove of palm trees with countless flying foxes, the herb garden and the Tropical Centre are all fascinating. *Daily 7am until sunset | rbgsyd.nsw.gov.au | City Rail Circular Quay, Martin Place or St James | 1 hr*

4 JUSTICE & POLICE MUSEUM

Are you in the mood for a little spookiness? Then pay a visit to the museum of Sydney's gangsters and crooks in the former home of the water police. The restored magistrates court, several remand cells and a collection of murder weapons, as well as artefacts belonging to the legendary Ned Kelly Gang are among the highlights. *Sat, Sun 10am–5pm | admission free | Albert St/Phillip St | short.travel/aus4 | bus/City Rail/ferry Circular Quay | 1 hr*

5 HARBOUR BRIDGE ★

Harbour Bridge is to Sydney what the Statue of Liberty is to New York. For generations of migrants, it was the much-longed-for sign that their journey was finally over: the symbol of freedom and new beginnings. In recent decades, it has above all been a magnet for travellers brave enough to climb the 1,332 steps of the outer arch of the bridge. The *Bridge Climb (from A$300 | 5 Cumberland Street, The Rocks | bridgeclimb.com)* may be expensive, but it's also an unforgettable experience. Make sure to book ahead!

INSIDER TIP
A small price for a great view

On a tight budget? For spectacular views of the city, harbour and Opera House, try the Pylon Lookout *(daily 10am–4pm | A$30, incl. Bridge Museum | Bridge Stairs, Cumberland St, The Rocks | pylonlookout.com.au)*. You can reach the Pylon from The Rocks.

6 THE ROCKS & BARANGAROO

★ The Rocks *(therocks.com)* at the western end of Circular Quay is the oldest part of Sydney. In 1788, convicts erected the city's first proper buildings on solid rock foundations. The sandstone structures that now line the quay and the narrow, cobbled streets date from the early to mid-19th century. In the 1970s, the historical buildings were slated to be demolished to make way for modern skyscrapers. The Builders Labourers' Federation, however, refused to knock them down. Today, The Rocks is a conservation area, and tourists have made the quarter their own – little wonder given the wonderful location close to Circular Quay and all its pubs and restaurants.

Visit the *Rocks Discovery Museum (daily 10am–5pm | admission free | 2–8 Kendall Lane | ½ hr)*, where Australia's history is traced to long before the European invasion, and at the weekend head to the *Market on George Street*. If you'd like to know more, a free 90-minute tour of The Rocks departs daily at 6pm from *Cadman's Cottage*

INSIDER TIP
Free tour

(110 George St). Spot the tour guides by their green T-shirt. *therocks.com | bus/City Rail/ferry Circular Quay*

A startling visual contrast is provided by the futuristic buildings in the new Barangaroo district. Dip into the gourmet offerings available along the attractive mile-long waterfront promenade. *Bus/City Rail/ferry Circular Quay*

7 ART GALLERY OF NEW SOUTH WALES

Amazingly, in 1874 – only a few decades after the transportation of the first convicts, and with a population of only 200,000 – a respectable art gallery opens in the middle of Sydney that is still one of the biggest in Australia today. Be sure to visit *Yiribana*, the world's largest exhibition of Aboriginal Australian art.

INSIDER TIP
Indigenous artists

Daily 10am–5pm | admission free, free guided tours on request | Art Gallery Rd, The Domain | artgallery.nsw.gov.au | Big Bus Sydney stop 7 | 1 hr

8 HYDE PARK BARRACKS

If walls could talk, then these ancient ones, built by convicts, would have plenty to say – probably not much of it uplifting, though. At least 50,000 convicts are said to have passed through the dismal gates, been inspected and assigned to work. After transportation of convicts ended in the second half of the 19th century, the building was used as an orphanage for Irish girls who had escaped the great famine. Their poignant stories live on in the moving museum. *Daily 10am–5pm | A$12 | Queens Sq/Macquarie St | short.travel/aus13 | Big Bus Sydney stop 11 | 1 hr*

The Justice & Police Museum reveals the dark side of the city's history

Watch sharks and turtles from below the waterline at the Sea Life Sydney Aquarium

9 AUSTRALIAN MUSEUM

Carnivorous giant kangaroos, monster wombats and dinosaurs with razor-sharp teeth – Sydney's natural history museum provides a fascinating and often humorous look at the evolutionary history of the Australian continent and its people and animals. *Daily 9.30am–5pm | admission free | 1 William St | australianmuseum.net.au | Big Bus Sydney stop 3 | 1 hr*

10 SYDNEY TOWER EYE

Did you know? Covering an area of more than 12,000km², Sydney is almost eight times the size of London. Very difficult to imagine – unless you happen to be standing 250m up, on the lookout platform of the Sydney Tower Eye, and gazing over the seemingly endless ocean of skyscrapers, detached homes and well-tended parks. That's all very nice, but where's the kick? That awaits on the *Skywalk*, a 45-minute tour around the tower, in the open air and partly on glass walkways. *Daily 9am–8pm | admission A$37, A$95 incl. Skywalk | access from the Centrepoint Shopping Centre, Level 5, 100 Market St | sydneytowereye.com.au | bus/City Rail St James | 1 hr*

11 DARLING HARBOUR ★

According to legend, the harbour shore was once known as The Hungry Mile, a reference to the waterside workers competing for work on the wharves each day. Hunger doesn't tend to be the problem today – unless, of course, you can resist the aromas wafting from the many and diverse restaurants. Darling Harbour also offers all kinds of entertainment, including a casino, IMAX cinema, the Aquarium, Wildlife World and Madame Tussauds wax museum. If you're travelling with children, make sure to reserve extra time for the water playground at the southern end of the harbour – the kids will never forgive you if you miss it! *darlingharbour.com | ferry from Circular Quay | Big Bus Sydney stops 16 and 17*

12 SEA LIFE SYDNEY AQUARIUM

The transparent tunnel takes you through an undersea world. The artificial Barrier Reef with its tropical fish and classical music is simply stunning. *Daily 9.30am–6pm | from A$56, online from A$53 | Aquarium Pier, Darling Harbour | sydneyaquarium.com.au | ferry Aquarium Pier | Big Bus Sydney stop 19 | 1½ hrs*

13 KINGS CROSS

Urban development has long since given this old Sydney neighbourhood an innocent look, but the legends of its rough past as a red-light district live on. Today "The Cross" is above all an entertainment centre for Sydneysiders who like to spend their evenings in popular pubs and nightclubs. However, it also offers backpackers' accommodation and inexpensive restaurants. *City Rail T4 Kings Cross*

14 TARONGA ZOO

Let's be honest: do giraffes really need this fabulous view? Maybe not, but it certainly makes for fantastic photographs: long giraffe necks at the front of the picture, the Opera House in the background. And when you do manage to drag your eyes away from the view, be sure to visit the flying display and the sea lions. *Daily 9.30am–5pm | A$53, online A$48 | Head Rd, Bradleys | taronga.org.au | ferry from Circular Quay (free in combination with a zoo ticket) | 2 hrs*

EATING & DRINKING

Where there are tourists, there is food: and you certainly won't be hungry for long at Darling Harbour or on Circular Quay, where you'll find one restaurant after another. You can fill up for slightly less in Kings Cross or in the suburbs Glebe, Newtown or Surry Hills. If you fancy seafood, don't miss a visit to *Sydney Fish Market (10am–5pm every day | Pyrmont Bridge Rd/Bank St | City Rail Fish Market)* for a delicious waterfront lunch of fresh prawns and oysters.

INSIDER TIP
Fresh out of the water

THE AUSTRALIAN

There's always a party going in this pub in the heart of The Rocks. In business since 1914, it's one of the oldest hostelries in Sydney. Tuck into an emu, kangaroo or crocodile pizza to accompany your craft beer – or opt for more conventional pub grub. *Daily from noon | 100 Cumberland St | tel. 02 92 47 22 29 | bus 311 Argyle Place | $$*

BAMBINI TRUST

Exquisite food and atmosphere, with coffee from Italy. The steaks and fresh seafood are a particular favourite with regulars. Tip: order a coffee to go and head for Albert Park close by. *Mon–Fri from 7am, Sat from 5.30pm | 185 Elizabeth St | tel. 02 92 83 70 98 | bambinitrust.com.au | City Rail Martin Place | $$$*

IL BARETTO

Not expensive and yet very good – Sydneysiders love such places, which means it is always packed at any time of day. Serves specialities from northern Italy as well as pasta dishes and pizzas. *Mon–Sat 5.30–9.30pm | 338 Oxford St | tel. 02 85 87 41 50 | bus 389 Paddington | $$*

HARRY'S CAFÉ DE WHEELS

Not exactly a location for gourmets, but oh-so Aussie: Harry's has been serving its famous pies for decades – with all sorts of Australian meat fillings as well as other variations. *Sun–Thu 10am–10pm, Fri/Sat until midnight | Tumbalong Park | tel. 02 83 46 41 00 | City Rail Town Hall | $*

LOVE.FISH

For the moment, this remains one of the few addresses in Barangaroo where the menu prices won't cause a sharp intake of breath. Taste freshly caught barramundi in coconut sauce or classic fish and chips. *Mon–Sat 11.30am–9pm, Sun 11.30am–4pm | 7/23 Barangaroo Av, Barangaroo | tel. 02 80 77 37 00 | lovefish.com.au | bus/City Rail Wynyard Station | $$*

LE FOOTE

No question, an Aussie barbecue in the garden with friends is the best! But in close second place is Le Foote, where you grill your steak yourself in the pub courtyard. There are tasty side dishes at the salad counter, plus plenty of beer on tap. *Mon/Tue 5–9pm, Wed–Sun noon–midnight | 101 George St, The Rocks | tel. 02 92 32 08 81 | bus/City Rail/ferry Circular Quay | $$*

INSIDER TIP
Grill party

MANTA

The decor is unpretentious – black wooden tables, white walls and few pictures. The same goes for the food: fresh oysters are served without any frills as is the Arab-style octopus. *Daily | The Wharf at Woolloomooloo, Cowper Wharf Rd | tel. 02 93 32 38 22 | bus 311 Potts Point | $$$*

SHOPPING

For the more stylish shoppers, the *Strand Arcade (255 Pitt St | City Rail Town Hall)* and the *Queen Victoria Building (455 George St | City Rail Town Hall)* house expensive boutiques, designer shops and tea rooms.

Unconventional fashions can be found on *King Street (bus 422 Newtown)* in Newtown and *Glebe Point Road (bus 433 near Hereford St)* in the student district of Glebe. Several top Australian designers have boutiques on *Oxford Street (bus 333 Darlinghurst Road)* in Paddington. This is also where the most popular *market* in the city is held every

The Australian has been a destination for thirsty pub-goers for more than 100 years

Saturday around St John's Church *(paddingtonmarkets.com.au)*. This is a great spot to pick up some nifty souvenirs from local artisans. Aboriginal art, everything from murals to boomerangs, is available from *Karlangu Aboriginal Art Centre (47 York St | karlangu.com | City Rail Wynyard)*.

SPORT & ACTIVITIES

You can easily leave the city behind you, even on foot, for example on the *Federation Cliff Walk*, a 5km path along the coast, from the eastern residential area of Dover Heights, past the sandstone cliffs to Watson Bay. If you're still feeling energetic, you can take the 6km *Coastal Walk* from Bondi to Coogee, or enjoy the views of *North Head Walk* in Manly. *short.travel/aus34*

Sydney is famous for its beautiful pools built into the sea, the oldest of which was built more than 200 years ago. Take a dip at *Bronte Baths* or *Cronulla Rock Pool* – both free of charge. A great fitness and wellness programme is on offer at the city-centre *Cook+Phillip Park Pool (daily 6am–8pm | pool entry A$8.70, fitness session A$24.80 | William St | cookand-phillip.org.au | City Rail St James)*.

BEACHES

Sydney's more than 30 beaches stretch almost 100km down the coast. *Bondi Beach*, the most famous and now on the National Heritage List, can be reached by bus, as can the other beaches *(transportnsw.info)*. There is less going on at *Tamarama*, *Bronte* and *Clovelly beaches*. *Coogee Beach* is

Start your night at the Lord Nelson

a pretty, family-friendly beach with hotels, restaurants and cafés. Some beaches also have rock pools, perfect for relaxing in, such as *Maroubra*, where you can treat yourself to a cup of coffee afterwards in *Pavilion Beachfront (daily | Fitzgerald Av | pavilionbeachfront.com.au)*. The waves at *Manly Beach* are up to 1.6m high. If you're not a strong swimmer, then take a few steps south to *Shelly Beach*, which is sheltered.

BALMORAL BEACH

This is the place to come if you want to avoid exposing your little ones to the rough east coast surf. To the north of the harbour, the bay of this pretty suburb is sheltered. While the kids build sandcastles, parents can soak in the view in comfort over lunch or a coffee at *Bathers' Pavilion (daily | tel. 02 99 69 50 50 | batherspavilion.com.au | $$$)*.

NIGHTLIFE

BARS & PUBS

The most typical watering holes are in *The Rocks*. *The Australian* *(see p. 49)*, *The Lord Nelson (19 Kent St)* and *The Argyle (12 Argyle St)* have remained unspoilt, the first two also serving their own delicious home-brewed beer. *Establishment Bar (248–252 George St | bus/City Rail/ferry Circular Quay)* on the ground floor of the eponymous boutique hotel is one of the hotspots of the "in" scene. There's often live music in the city's oldest pub, the *Fortune of War (137 George St | City Rail/ferry Circular Quay)* on Thursday to Sunday evenings.

CASINO

Casinos are hugely popular in Australia. Experience the magic for yourself as you stand in front of the glittering entrance to the *Star Casino* and its shopping arcade. *80 Pyrmont St | star.com.au | Big Bus Sydney stop 15*

NIGHTCLUBS

Nightlife centres on *Oxford Street* and the neighbouring districts of *Paddington* and *Kings Cross*. Clubs that are often open until around 5am, especially at weekends, include *Kinselas (383 Bourke St | bus 389 near Burton St), Noir Sydney (163–169 Oxford St | bus 333 Taylor Sq), Oxford Hotel (134 Oxford St | bus 333 Oxford St, corner of Darlinghurst Rd).*

OPEN-AIR CINEMA

Australians love open-air cinemas. In Sydney these are *Westpac Open Air Cinema (Mrs Macquarie's Chair | Jan/Feb | A$39 | westpacopenair.com.au)* in the Royal Botanic Garden; *Moonlight Cinema (Centennial Park | Dec–Mar | A$25 | moonlight.com.au | City Rail Bondi Junction);* and *Sunset Cinema (Millet St, North Sydney | Jan–April | A$27 | sunsetcinema.com.au),* where picnics are allowed.

THEATRE

Belvoir Street Theatre (25 Belvoir St | tel. 02 96 99 34 44 | belvoir.com.au | City Rail Central Station) is a leading theatre company that has produced the likes of Mel Gibson. Experience dance, drama, music, and comedy at the *Roslyn Packer Theatre (22 Hickson Rd, Walsh Bay, Millers Point | tel. 02 92 50 19 99 | roslynpackertheatre.com.au | bus/City Rail/ferry Circular Quay).*

At the *Opera House* *(see p. 45)* you can see opera, comedy, dance and theatre *(box office 02 92 50 71 11).*

Lifeguards are always at the ready on Sydney's beaches

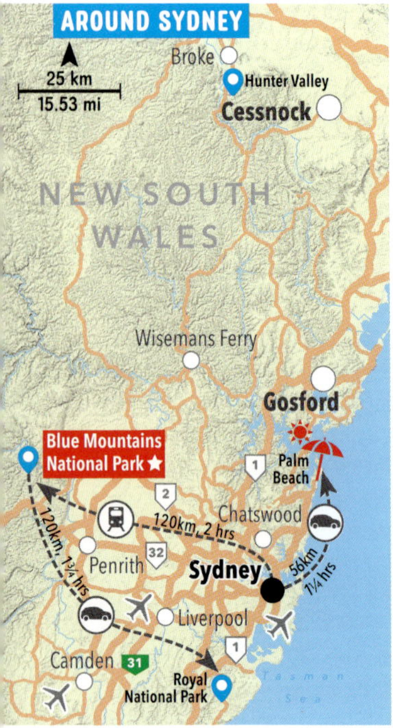

AROUND SYDNEY

ROYAL NATIONAL PARK

36km / 50 mins from Sydney by car

It's hard to believe you're at the gateway to a city of millions. After Yellowstone in California, "The Royal" was the second national park to be established in the world – a fabulous haven of nature that is just a little smaller than Liechtenstein. Countless walking trails meander through the bush and forests, the cliffs falling steeply down to the ocean. *The Royal National Park Visitor Centre (2 Lady Carrington Drive, Audley | tel. 02 95 42 06 48)* has information on hiking trails and other activities. Travel here by *Cronulla Ferries (A$9/10 | cronullaferries.com.au)* to Bundeena. *Daily 7am–8.30pm | National Park fee A$12/car and day | short.travel/aus35 |* *J6*

BLUE MOUNTAINS NATIONAL PARK ★

120km / 2 hrs from Sydney by train and bus

The wild Blue Mountains start west of Sydney. The Three Sisters, an impressive rock formation near the little town of Katoomba, are of considerable spiritual importance to the local Aboriginal people. Wonderful views over deep gorges and the forested mountain ranges in the national park can be had from Echo Point, not far from the spectacular Three Sisters.

Just 1km or so away on the western outskirts of Katoomba, *Scenic World (daily 9am–5pm | from A$54 for the all-inclusive Unlimited Discovery Pass | scenicworld.com.au)* combines breathtaking views with a bit of excitement. The more daring can take the *Scenic Railway* that plunges 415m down a steep incline, then the *Scenic Skyway*, a cablecar across the gorge far below, or the *Scenic Cableway*, another panoramic cablecar ride, and hike the well-maintained 3km *Scenic Walkway* through the rainforest.

Information and maps are available from the *NPWS Blue Mountains Heritage Centre (Govetts Leap Rd, Blackheath | tel. 02 47 87 88 77 | visit bluemountains.com.au)*. Various bus companies run day trips from Sydney. If you arrive by train from *Central Station (transportnsw.info)*, you can take the *Blue Mountains Explorer Bus (explorerbus.com.au)* that starts at Katoomba and stops at the major sights. 🕮 H6

PALM BEACH

56km / 1¼ hrs from Sydney by car

This is where the other half live. A good hour's drive north of the city centre is the suburb of Palm Beach, on a headland stretching out into the sea. Particularly beautiful and usually far less crowded than beaches closer to the city is the *beach* directly south of Barrenjoey Lighthouse. While you're in this neck of the woods, stop for a short *walk* in the idyllic *Ku-ring-gai Chase National Park*, where you'll find (rain)forest and heathland galore. 🕮 J6

HUNTER VALLEY

120km / 2 hrs from Sydney by car

The Hunter Valley is the oldest wine-growing region in Australia with more than 150 award-winning wineries *(winecountry.com.au)*, producing delicate, fruity white wines and some reds (Pinot Noir and Shiraz). Many wineries also have first-class restaurants – and luxurious accommodation. 🕮 H–J6

SLEEP WELL IN SYDNEY

CITY CAMPING

Cockatoo Island (tel. 02 97 00 41 11 | cockatooisland.gov.au | ferry Circular Quay, Barangaroo | $-$$$) rises up from the harbour. The islet was once a meeting place for the Indigenous Wareamah people; later it was used as a prison and a shipyard. Today, it's part of the cityscape. There are various places to stay on the island, including the renovated rooms of the former fire station. The Garden Riverview Apartments have terraces and barbecues. There are also permanent tents installed, with views over the water.

LUXURY BACKPACKING WITH A HARBOUR VIEW

Admittedly, this isn't really budget travel, but what is more popular in Sydney than the impressive view of the Opera House and harbour? At *Sydney Harbour YHA (106 rooms | 110 Cumberland St | tel. 02 82 72 09 00 | yha.com.au | bus/City Rail/ferry Circular Quay | $$)*, you can enjoy the view and a breeze from the deckchairs on the roof terrace of this luxury hostel, with its comfortable dorms and double rooms with en-suite bathrooms, large clean kitchen and inviting common rooms. Book well in advance!

NEW SOUTH WALES

A LITTLE BIT OF EVERYTHING

Endless beaches, eucalyptus forests around romantic lakes, isolated farms and cattle stations, subtropical heat in huge national parks that encompass landscapes ranging from desert to rainforest, and freezing temperatures in the Snowy Mountains – all this is New South Wales.

The "First State", at 801,600km² and more than three times the size of the UK, is the oldest and most densely populated state in Australia – although outside Sydney, with its population of

Experience the intense greenery of the rainforest in Dorrigo National Park

five million, you don't really notice this. There are lots of empty beaches along its 1,000km-long coastline; you can hike for days in the Snowy Mountains without ever meeting a soul, and in the pubs in the outback, strangers are still something of a novelty. For many visitors who land at Sydney Airport, the fascinating state capital overshadows the "rest" of New South Wales. But the state has a lot more going for it.

NEW SOUTH WALES

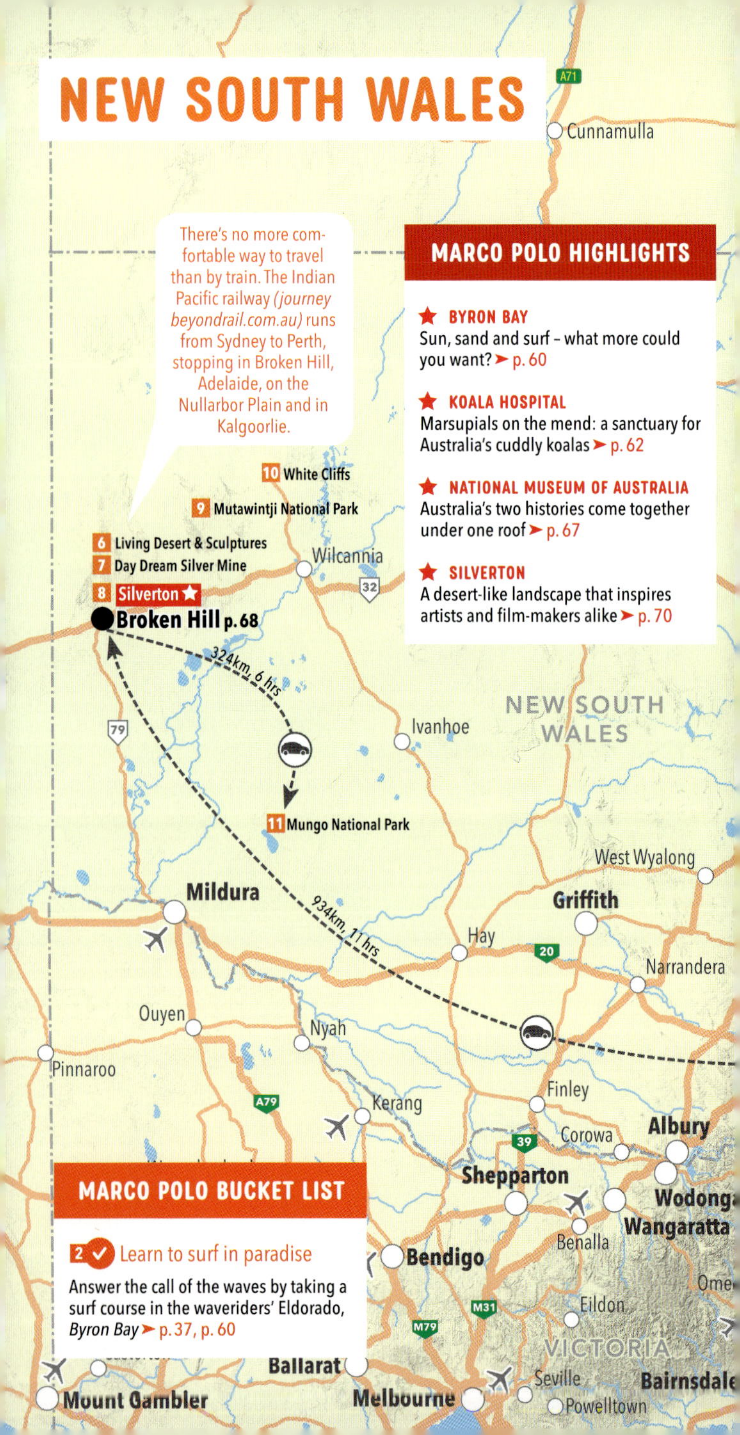

MARCO POLO HIGHLIGHTS

★ **BYRON BAY**
Sun, sand and surf – what more could you want? ➤ p. 60

★ **KOALA HOSPITAL**
Marsupials on the mend: a sanctuary for Australia's cuddly koalas ➤ p. 62

★ **NATIONAL MUSEUM OF AUSTRALIA**
Australia's two histories come together under one roof ➤ p. 67

★ **SILVERTON**
A desert-like landscape that inspires artists and film-makers alike ➤ p. 70

MARCO POLO BUCKET LIST

2 ✓ Learn to surf in paradise

Answer the call of the waves by taking a surf course in the waveriders' Eldorado, *Byron Bay* ➤ p. 37, p. 60

QUEENSLAND
Tara
Toowoomba
Brisbane
Ipswich
Gold Coast
Millmerran
St George
Warwick
Tweed Heads
Mount Warning 1
Watego's Beach
Goondiwindi
Lismore
Byron Bay ★
p.60
Do you want to learn how to surf? Those in the know rate the waves at The Pass beach near Byron Bay as perfect for beginners, especially between April and September.
Yamba
Moree
Grafton
Woolgoolga
Walgett
Narrabri
Dorrigo National Park 2
Coffs Harbour
Armidale
Macksville
Gunnedah
Tamworth
Koala Hospital ★
Port Macquarie
p.62
Gilgandra
Scone
Taree
Dubbo
Singleton
Seal Rocks
Mudgee
771km, 8½ hrs
Cessnock
Newcastle
If you visit in September or October, then check out the colourful flower carpet that decorates the capital as part of the Floriade Festival.
Doyalson
Gosford
Penrith
Sydney
Tasman Sea
Liverpool
Wollongong
4 Kiama
Yass
Jervis Bay National Park 3
Canberra
National Museum of Australia ★
Queanbeyan
Pebbly Beach
227km, 4 hrs
Hyams Beach
Batemans Bay
p.63
Cooma
Trains and buses between Sydney and Melbourne travel along the inland route. Only Premier MS buses (premierms.com.au) serve the route south from Sydney to Eden, with plenty of stops at beautiful beaches on the Sapphire Coast.
5 Snowy Mountains National Park
Tathra
Bombala
Eden
Mallacoota
100 km
62.13 mi

BYRON BAY

(▯ J5) **A wealth of water sports, a beautiful hinterland with high mountains and rainforest, as well as a lively pub scene make ★ Byron Bay (pop. 10,900) a booming tourist destination.**

This was once the preserve of backpackers and dropouts – but they have long since moved further inland to Nimbin. It is largely young, well-heeled tourists who really get things going in the evenings on Bay Street, while during the day ✓ surfers enjoy stunning wide beaches. *Main Beach* stretches 50km, almost as far as the Gold Coast in Queensland, while *Watego's Beach* is a dream come true for surfers who ride the breakers alongside dolphins.

SIGHTSEEING

CAPE BYRON

This peninsula, named by James Cook on his first trip (1768–71), juts out a long way into the sea. You can drive to the old lighthouse or take the well-maintained path to *Captain Cook Lookout* (3.5km, the entire round trip will take about two hours). From here you have an overwhelming view of Watego's Bay. June and July, and September to November are the best months for whale watching; dolphins play in the water all year round.

Surfers at Byron Bay don't have to wait long for the perfect wave

EATING & DRINKING

THE SMOKING CAMEL

Find the flavours of the Middle East in this colourful restaurant, which serves tasty falafel, houmous and steaks seasoned with *baharat*. There are good-value cocktails during happy hour (5–6pm). *Daily from 5pm | 3/17 Lawson St | tel. 04 84 36 21 18 | thesmokingcamel.com | $$*

THAI LUCY

This place has been serving the best Thai cuisine in the area since the 1990s. It's handily located a short hop from Main Beach. *Daily | 2/4 Bay Lane | tel. 02 66 80 80 83 | thailucy.com | $$*

AROUND BYRON BAY

The area inland from Byron Bay is fascinating and varied, with banana plantations, dense rainforest and small villages that have an appealing mixture of unconventional shops. From Byron Bay, head first of all for *Mullumbimby*, then take the highway to *Murwillumbah (approx. 50km)*. From here, the roads to *Uki*, *Nimbin*, *Lismore* and the little artists' colony *Bangalow* are narrow and twisty.

1 MOUNT WARNING

70km / 1 hr from Byron Bay by car

The turning to *Mount Warning National Park (mtwarning.net)* is between Murwillumbah and Uki. *Mount Warning* is the remnant of a huge volcano that erupted millions of years ago. A unique ecological niche was created between the lava masses, and wonderful rainforest and rare flora and fauna now thrive.

INSIDER TIP Up the volcano

It is well worth climbing Mount Warning early in the morning when the sun starts to rise above Australia's easternmost point and the surrounding area is bathed in a mesmerising light. The tour takes about two hours. Note: the final section should only be tackled if you have a head for heights. Sturdy footwear essential. J5

PORT MACQUARIE

(□ J6) **Considering the heavenly beaches, it is almost impossible to imagine that this idyllic beachside town was once a penal settlement for convicts who were repeat offenders.**

"Port" (pop. 52,000) is one of the oldest settlements in Australia. It's a manageable small town that nestles against the Hasting River, and offers a wide range of water sports, with mile-long beaches for swimming or surfing, stretching from *Town Beach* and *Oxley Beach* near the town centre to *Lighthouse Beach* in the south.

SIGHTSEEING

KOALA HOSPITAL ★

One of the largest animal hospitals of its kind in Australia , this volunteer-run facility often has more than 30 patients. Many of the koalas taken in here are victims of road accidents or bush fires. After being treated by expert vets and when they have fully recovered, they are released back into the wild. If you're still looking for that special souvenir, how about adopting a koala? Sadly, you don't actually get to take the bear home, but you do get a certificate complete with a picture of your koala (who will be released back into the wild after treatment), with your donation going to the Koala Hospital. Feeding time is at 3pm. *Daily 8am–4.30pm | admission A$12.50, children A$8 | Lord St | koalahospital.org.au | 1 hr*

INSIDER TIP
Adopt a koala!

SEA ACRES RAINFOREST CENTRE

Discover the rainforest. The 1.3km boardwalk – supposedly the longest wooden walk in the world – is up to 7m above the ground, and it takes you through an unspoilt tropical rainforest at eye level with a whole range of tree-dwellers. *Daily 9am–4.30pm | A$9 | Sea Acres Nature Reserve | short.travel/aus7 | 1½ hrs*

HASTINGS RIVER

A solid proportion of the oysters sold in Australia are farmed in the waters of Port Macquarie. Some cruises stop at the oyster farms, and dolphins frolic in the water all year round. If you're there between June and September, make sure your camera's to hand for any whale sightings. Join *Port Jet Cruise Adventures (from A$30 | 1 Short St, Town Wharf | tel. 65 83 88 11 | portjet.com.au)* onboard; if you're hungry, book the trip that serves up fish and chips *(A$50)*.

EATING & DRINKING

PORT FRESH SEAFOODS

This is where you can find cheap fresh oysters, and other delicacies. *Mon–Fri 9am–5.30pm, Sat 9am–2pm | 5/23–41 Short St | tel. 02 65 83 83 48 | portfreshseafoods.com.au*

Cute animal portraits are guaranteed at the Koala Hospital

AROUND PORT MACQUARIE

2 DORRIGO NATIONAL PARK

175km / 2 hrs from Port Macquarie by car

The park is 900m up in the mountains of the Great Dividing Range, 180km north of Port Macquarie. It is one of the most beautiful and accessible national parks in New South Wales. The 70m-high skywalk, a 250m-long path through the tree canopy of the rainforest, can be especially recommended. Pick up a fold-out map with all the trails marked at the *Dorrigo Rainforest Centre (daily 9am–4.30pm | Dome Rd | short.travel/aus37)*. A number of artists, craftspeople and organic farmers have settled in and around the pretty historical village of *Bellingen* (pop. 13,000). Good craft shops and a nice café can be found in the *Old Butter Factory (1 Doepel St | theoldbutterfactory.com.au)*. J5

BATEMANS BAY

(H7) **Even travellers need a break at some point! And where would be better to stop and relax than idyllic Batemans Bay (pop. 17,500) on the south coast?**

This idyllic sunbathing spot is a good starting point for exploring the hidden beaches, fishing villages and national parks along the south coast.

SIGHTSEEING

MURRAMURANG NATIONAL PARK

Now this is what you call down under: a tent under the eucalyptus trees, endless, empty beaches and adorable pygmy kangaroos, far more curious than shy, who will happily jump over to meet you – and all just a 20-minute drive from the seaside town of Batemans Bay. The national park runs along a spectacular stretch of coast with small sandy beaches, steep cliffs and numerous caves. Hikers and fossil hunters in particular will definitely find what they are looking for here. At *Pebbly Beach*, a small, sheltered beach inside the national park, your chances of meeting a pygmy kangaroo are high!

EATING & DRINKING

STARFISH DELI

Incredible food with an even better view at this fish and pizza restaurant right on the water. *Daily 9am–8pm | Clyde St | tel. 02 44 72 48 80 | $$–$$$*

AROUND BATEMANS BAY

3 JERVIS BAY NATIONAL PARK

115km / 1½ hrs from Batemans Bay by car

North of Batemans Bay is this idyllic bay with bright white beaches, crystal-clear water, eucalyptus forests and pockets of rainforest. Kangaroos, wallabies and flying foxes can be seen almost everywhere. Parrots land on the arms and shoulders of anyone who has food with them. Dolphins and penguins live in the sheltered bays. If that weren't enough, whale-watching is possible from May to November: *Dolphin Watch Cruises (from A$52, A$75 in whale season | 50 Owen St, Huskisson | tel. 02 44 41 63 11 | dolphinwatch.com.au)*. Just so you know, Jervis Bay boasts the whitest sandy beach – not just in Australia, but allegedly in the world, with *Hyams Beach* even making it into the book of Guinness World Records. H6–7

INSIDER TIP **Snow-white sand**

4 KIAMA

160km / 4 hrs from Batemans Bay by car

The pretty, historical part of this town (pop. 15,000), north of Batemans Bay, follows the rugged cliffs along the coast to *Blowhole*, Kiama's special attraction. And if the weather is right, it really is quite something: when the wind comes from the southwest, the waves crashing against the cliffs are forced through a deep underwater cavern and shoot 60m up through a hole in the rock. H6

5 SNOWY MOUNTAINS NATIONAL PARK

317km / 4 hrs from Batemans Bay by car

Welcome to Australia's answer to the Alps! The mountains rising in the

See Australian politics in action in Parliament House in Canberra

hinterland above the south coast are only ever visited by a few foreign tourists. The Snowies, however, are not just a magnet for winter-sports enthusiasts. In summer, you can experience the solitude of the mountains in this huge national park, the likes of which you won't find in Europe. A large part of the "Australian Alps", which stretch as far as Victoria, is a protected area (in New South Wales at the *Mount Kosciuszko National Park*, in Victoria at the *Alpine National Park*). The tourist centres are *Cooma*, *Thredbo* and *Jindabyne*.

An unforgettable experience is a ride through the outlying areas of the national park over a period of several days, organised by *Snowy River Horseback Tours (2 days from A$750 | snowyrivertours.com)*. 🕮 H7

CANBERRA

(🕮 117) **Canberra (pop. 450,000) is the result of a compromise between Sydney and Melbourne after they could not agree on which city should become the capital.**

It was literally built in the middle of nowhere. "Canberry" – the meeting place – was what the Aboriginal people called the area. The American architects Walter Burley Griffin and Marion Mahony Griffin won the commission to build the city in 1912. Canberra is characterised by its strict geometrical design. The city itself and its suburbs cover about a quarter of the 2,400km² of the total area in the Australian Capital Territory (ACT), which does not belong to the state of

New South Wales, but has its own administration. Canberra has two hearts: the northern district around *London Circuit* and the southern one around *Capital Hill*, where Parliament House stands. A trip to *Mount Ainslie Lookout* provides the best picture of the city. From there you can see the parliamentary district. Interestingly, just a few minutes from the government district is the *Red Hill Nature Reserve*. It's not unusual to spot wild kangaroos out here, where nature is certainly in charge.

SIGHTSEEING

NATIONAL FILM & SOUND ARCHIVE

The archive is home to key film and audio recordings from the late 19th century onwards. Once you've seen the main exhibition, pop into the small theatre room for fascinating historic short films as well as old cinema and TV classics – all free of charge! *Daily 10am–4pm, Fri 10am–8pm | admission free | McCoy Circuit, Acton Peninsula | nfsa.gov.au | 1½ hrs*

Experiments and discoveries for scientists large and small in the Questacon

NATIONAL GALLERY OF AUSTRALIA

Do not miss this opportunity to see 5,000 years of international art and an excellent collection of Aboriginal Australian works, some up to 30,000 years old. Check out Sidney Nolan's Ned Kelly collection – a central piece of modern Australian art history. *Daily 10am–5pm | admission free | Parkes Place | nga.gov.au |* *1½ hrs*

NATIONAL MUSEUM OF AUSTRALIA ★

From Aboriginal traditions and Australian fauna to Vegemite – this eye-catching museum is dedicated to Australia's diverse cultures. The interwoven steel "ropes" outside represent the numerous stories that make up the country. *Daily 9am–5pm | admission free | Lawson Crescent, Acton Peninsula | nma.gov.au |* *2 hrs*

PARLIAMENT HOUSE

Parliament House is home to the two national houses of parliament, the House of Representatives, which sits in the green chamber, and the Senate, which has a red colour scheme. The 8m flagpole on the roof has become the symbol of Canberra. Built at a cost of A$1.1 billion, the building – which was opened in 1988 – is one of the largest in the Southern Hemisphere. As well as the government, it houses more than 3,000 works of art, many of which are in rooms that are open to the public. Free guided tours *(several daily | tel. 02 62 77 53 99)* can be booked there and then. A visit is particularly interesting at Question Time. Shouting and aggressive remarks between Government and Opposition members are not unusual. Information on sessions is available on the website *aph.gov.au.* *1½ hrs*

QUESTACON

This is an absolute must for (budding) scientists or just anyone keen on experiments and testing things out. The science and technology centre offers the chance to experience an earthquake, admire how lightning strikes or trigger a tsunami. *Daily 9am–5pm | A$25, children A$19 | King Edward Terrace | questacon.edu.au |* *2 hrs*

EATING & DRINKING

AKIBA

Don't put yourself through the misery of trying to choose; instead, ask for the "Just Feed Me" eight-course meal (vegetarian version also available) with freshly prepared Asian creations. Very popular, so it's a good idea to book in advance! *Daily | 40 Bunda St | tel. 02 61 62 06 02 | akiba.com.au | $$*

BENTSPOKE

Don't let anyone tell you that nothing ever happens in Canberra. In this hip brewery pub, you'll see an award-winning crankshaft, and dine on excellent salads, burgers and other pub fare. *Daily | 38 Mort St, Braddon | tel. 02 62 57 52 20 | bentspokebrewing.com.au | $$*

Explore the Living Desert & Sculptures park just outside Broken Hill

NIGHTLIFE

Restaurants and pubs line the modern developed foreshore in the suburb of *Kingston*, so you can enjoy a pleasant stroll from drink to drink along the shore. Braddon has become a hip if slightly small nightlife area.

THE DOCK

Tempura oysters, lychee Martinis, football and live music – the new dock on the banks of Lake Burley Griffin combines the rough Aussie pub atmosphere with class. *Daily | 7 Giles St | thedockkingston.com.au*

HIPPO CO

Famous for the best Martinis in town. The proprietors also have a soft spot for good live jazz *(Wed)*. Try the bar's own fruity cocktail creation, the *Rye-Ball*, or, for something stronger, the *barrel-aged Negroni* – both in-house recipes. *Closed Sun | 17 Garema Place | hippo.com.au*

BROKEN HILL

(G6) **When driving along the highway, Broken Hill (pop. 17,000) suddenly appears out of nowhere: an urban oasis in a desert-like environment.**

This prosperous small town, over 1,100km from Sydney, owes its existence to a farm labourer from Stuttgart in Germany: in 1883, Charles Rasp came across a lode of lead, silver and zinc, which proved to be one of the most lucrative in the world. The slightly collapsed hill – hence the name Broken Hill – became the site of one of the biggest mines, operated by the *Broken Hill Proprietary Company (BHP)*, which became the world's biggest mining company. Despite intensive mining, the reserves are by no means exhausted. *Silver City*, as Broken Hill likes to boast, has a lively art scene and great attractions (including an extremely interesting Flying Doctor base).

Here, by the way, you'll have to adjust your watch. Although the town is in New South Wales, it is in the South Australian time zone.

SIGHTSEEING

LINE OF LODE MINERS MEMORIAL

This memorial to the hundreds of workers who died in the mine is in a fitting location on Federation Hill above the town. Good views, an informative visitor centre and a café. *Daily 6am–9pm | admission free | ½ hr*

EATING & DRINKING

BELLS

The retro milk bar has survived since the 1950s and unflinchingly continues to serve all sorts of flavours of non-alcoholic milkshakes and soda spiders (ice-cream floats), as well as ice cream and coffee specialities. *Daily 10am–5.30pm | 160 Patton St | in the south of the town | tel. 08 80 87 53 80*

SHOPPING

ARTS & CRAFTS

There are so many *art galleries* and *craft shops* in Broken Hill that you can spend days visiting studios and exhibitions here. A list of addresses and contacts is available from the visitor centre.

The "Flying Doctor artist" Howard W Steer's bright and colourful paintings are typical, and his work can be found at 721 William Street *(howardsteerart.com.au)*. *Pro Hart Gallery (Mon–Sat 9am–5pm | A$5 | 108 Wyman St | prohart.com.au)* exhibits (and sells) works by the local artist Kevin Charles Hart, who died in 2006; it also offers art classes.

AROUND BROKEN HILL

6 LIVING DESERT & SCULPTURES

12km / ¼ hr from Broken Hill by car

This modern sculpture park is out in the desert, at the top of a hill and far enough from the lights of the town to show off the colours to their best, especially at sunset. It's about a 20-minute walk from the car park; there is a pay office at the entrance *(A$6 per person; please have the right change). Daily 8.30am–8pm | 1 hr |* *G6*

INSIDER TIP **Art at dusk**

Mad Max once parked here! Silverton is a popular film location

7 DAY DREAM SILVER MINE

31km / 40 mins from Broken Hill by car

A lot of the history here is actually underground. A guided tour (sturdy shoes necessary) through the narrow, low galleries gives you an impression of the hard and dangerous work in the mine at the end of the 19th century, when even children were sent underground. *Tours daily 10am and 11.30am | A$33 | turning signposted off the road to Silverton | daydreammine.com.au | 1½ hrs | G6*

8 SILVERTON ★

24km / 25 mins from Broken Hill by car

A bizarre near-ghost town from the days when silver was mined on a grand scale here. However, there are still people here, and you'll meet them in the little-changed pub of *Silverton Hotel ($$)*, in the small café and the unconventional artist studios which have been set up in the deserted buildings and are well worth a visit. Your walk through this dusty place should also include the old cemetery with its marble gravestones.

Silverton is a familiar name in the world of film: the outback setting was used for classic films such as *Mad Max II* and *Priscilla, Queen of the Desert*, among others. At the *Mundi Mundi Plains*, 7km away (signposted), you look out over an amazingly wide horizon. Rumour has it the view here can stretch so far into the distance you can even see the curvature of the earth. In any case, you can't deny it's a pretty impressive panorama! G6

9 MUTAWINTJI NATIONAL PARK

174km / 3½ hrs from Broken Hill by car

This nature reserve, spanning almost 70,000 hectares, is home to a wealth of cave paintings and petroglyphs left behind by local Aboriginal people. Background information is available in the *Cultural Centre*. Access is via an unpaved road; you can pitch your tent on the *Homestead Campground (short.travel/aus5)* which has a small kiosk. A guided day trip in a 4WD from Broken Hill with *Tri State Safaris (A$230 | tristate.com.au)* can be recommended. *G5*

10 WHITE CLIFFS

286km / 3 hrs from Broken Hill by car

Opal seekers have turned this area northeast of Broken Hill into a lunar landscape where life is largely spent underground in the cool and shade. After all, temperatures in summer are known to climb above the 40°C mark. See for yourself what it's like to live underground by staying in dug-out accommodation. Opals and opal jewellery can be found at *Red Earth Opal (100 Dug Out St)*, and they also offer mine tours *(daily 3pm | A$35 | redearthopal.com)*. *G5*

11 MUNGO NATIONAL PARK

324km / 5¾ hrs from Broken Hill by car

According to archaeologists, this national park, measuring some 280km², could be one of the cradles of mankind. Archaeological finds bear witness to long-extinct animals and prehistoric human beings. The remains of "Mungo Man" and "Mungo Lady", who were believed to have roamed this patch of earth over 42,000 years ago, were unearthed here.

The landscape's main attraction is the *Walls of China*, picturesque formations of sand and clay. Some of the roads in this area are dirt tracks in places.

For information, including on guided tours and accommodation, visit the website *short.travel/aus58*. The *Visitor Centre* at the southwest entrance to the park is not always open. *G6*

SLEEP WELL IN NEW SOUTH WALES

A LODGE WITH A WILD SIDE

The prices may be a little steep, but this is a once-in-a-lifetime experience. You'll stay in the safari-inspired *Jamala Wildlife Lodge (8 rooms | 999 Lady Denman Drive, Canberra | tel. 02 62 87 84 44 | jamalawildlifelodge.com.au | $$$)*, where only a glass wall separates you from the lion or bear sanctuary. Tours of the zoo, meals and drinks are included.

SLEEP UNDER THE STARS

During the day, you share the beach with a bunch of curious kangaroos, and at night, with the Milky Way. Unroll your sleeping bag in the open air under the eucalyptus trees at *Mystery Bay Campground (190 Mystery Bay Rd, 16km south of Narooma | tel. 04 28 62 23 57 | mysterybaycampground.com.au | $)* and let the surf lull you to sleep.

VICTORIA

GOLD, WAVES & APOSTLES

Victoria is Australia in miniature. Compared to other states, it's a manageable region in which you'll find nearly all the variety that the vast landmass of Australia has to offer.

Footpaths along rugged cliffs, broad surf beaches, snow-covered peaks, lonely deserts, gold deposits and gourmet restaurants. What more could you want? The multicultural metropolis of Melbourne is the heart of the second-smallest federal state and – according to various rankings – one of the best cities in the world to live in.

The name may be misleading but the view of the Twelve Apostles is undeniably dramatic

Take time to immerse yourself in its vibrant art scene, high-energy sporting events, café culture and cocktail bars.

But make sure you also travel beyond its boundaries: to visit the Grampians National Park with its ancient rock paintings; to see the penguins on Phillip Island and the wombats in Wilsons Promontory National Park; and, of course, to travel along the world's most famous coastal route – the Great Ocean Road.

VICTORIA
Wedderburn
St Arnaud
Inglewood
Murtoa
Bendigo
VICTORIA
M79
Maryborough
Castlemaine
Stawell
Avoca
Grampians
p. 85
Ararat
The Grampians are at their most impressive in spring, when the mountain meadows are filled with wildflowers. But there's a chance you'll see a kangaroo outside your hotel or your tent at any time of year …
Beaufort
Creswick
Daylesford
M8
Ballarat
Ballan
Buninyong
273km, 4½ hrs
Bannockburn
Mortlake
Terang
Cobden
Warrnambool
M1
Colac
Anglesea
Lorne
Bay of Martyrs
Port Campbell
5 Port Campbell National Park
Great Otway National Park 4
3 Apollo Bay
30 km
18.64 mi

MARCO POLO HIGHLIGHTS

★ **FEDERATION SQUARE**
The largest collection of Australian art is housed in this controversial development ➤ p. 76

★ **ROYAL BOTANIC GARDENS**
Sport, concerts and bats in Melbourne's "green lung" ➤ p. 78

★ **MELBOURNE MUSEUM**
Find out about the history and culture of the First Peoples of Victoria and Australia ➤ p. 79

★ **PHILLIP ISLAND**
Tiny penguins in their best dress coats march up the beach every evening ➤ p. 83

★ **PORT CAMPBELL NATIONAL PARK**
See the famous Twelve Apostles for yourself ➤ p. 85

★ **GRAMPIANS**
Wake up and meet the kangaroo outside your tent ➤ p. 85

MELBOURNE

(🕮 G7) **First came fortune seekers in the Gold Rush, later refugees and migrants in search of a better future. People from more than 140 nations have transformed Melbourne (pop. 5.2 million) into a thriving microcosm that celebrates its colourful cultural heritage with more relish than probably anywhere else in the world.**

You can enjoy bratwurst at the local Oktoberfest, halwa during Indian Diwali, and dumplings for Chinese New Year. No wonder the menus in the thousand restaurants offer literally everything, from Mediterranean and Tibetan to Jamaican cuisine. And, although the City of Diversity clings obstinately to traditional customs from all over the world, Melbourne simply is, and always will be, seriously cool and trendy.

WHERE TO START?

Federation Square is the perfect starting point for visitors as this is where the Information Centre and several interesting museums can be found. Flinders Street Station is on the west side of the square and it's only a short walk across Princes Bridge to the Southbank complex with good restaurants, casino and the Eureka Tower. Whatever you do, don't try to drive into the centre: parking spaces are hard to find, and the car parks are expensive.

Lose yourself in the many alleys and arcades of the city, or enjoy the vast, well-looked-after parks such as the *Royal Botanic Gardens* or *Carlton Gardens*. Getting around is no problem: public transport within the square mile of the centre is free. The *City Circle Tram (ptv.vic.gov.au)* runs through the centre every ten minutes daily between 10am and 6pm.

SIGHTSEEING

Make the most of the *Melbourne Greeter Service (tel. 03 96 58 96 58 | short.travel/aus59)* and book a free two- to four-hour *city walk* for up to four people. Tours leave daily at 10am from Federation Square /Visitor Centre.

FEDERATION SQUARE ★

A landmark square and cultural hub. The angled façades and crooked corners of this giant, modern museum and restaurant complex on the banks of the Yarra is not only eye-catching, but also an important setting for Melbourne's jam-packed calendar of events. The pointed, glass-fronted, zinc-clad building is home to the *Ian Potter Centre: NGV Australia*, which is dedicated to Australian art; its displays include an excellent collection of ancient and modern Aboriginal art. *Daily 11am–6pm | admission free | fedsq.com | ⏲ 3 hrs*

IMMIGRATION MUSEUM

Experience up close how difficult life was for people who came to Australia in search of a better life or fleeing from war and persecution. The museum

also highlights current immigration issues. *Daily 9am–5pm | A$15 | 400 Flinders St | museumvictoria.com.au/immigrationmuseum |* ⏲ *1½ hrs*

SEALIFE AQUARIUM

You might not spot the leafy sea dragon, disguised as seaweed, in its small aquarium straight away. Cool, yes, but not quite the size you might expect a dragon to be. This is not the case with the sharks, swordfish and rays – you can experience these sea creatures up close from the transparent tunnel. However, the uncontested stars are, without doubt, the king penguins, which slide awkwardly over the ice or roll playfully into the water. *Daily 9am–6pm | A$51, cheaper online | Flinders St/King St | visitsealife.com |* ⏲ *2 hrs*

MELBOURNE SKYDECK

You won't believe how quickly you'll be whisked to the top of the *Melbourne Tower*, the city's tallest building. It takes only 40 seconds to reach the 88th floor. There are 360-degree panoramic views of the city's skyscrapers and far beyond. If you want to get the adrenaline flowing, then step onto *The Edge (A$43 incl. entrance to Skydeck)*, an all-glass cube 300m above the ground. The glass changes from opaque to clear at the touch of a button – a dizzying and surprising effect. *Daily 10am–10pm | from A$31 | Riverside Quay | melbourneskydeck.com.au |* ⏲ *1 hr*

SOUTHBANK

Wander over the bridge from Federation Square and you'll be on

Melbourne's favourite stretch of riverside. Here you'll find a large shopping complex, the *Crown Casino* and some renowned arts and cultural venues. The *Arts Centre Melbourne (artscentremelbourne.com.au)* stages all kinds of music, theatre and comedy.

SHRINE OF REMEMBRANCE

Built to commemorate the Australians who lost their lives in the two World Wars, this temple-like construction is something all local schoolchildren visit. The country sent more than 415,000 soldiers to Europe in World War I, 60,000 of whom fell – a serious figure for a nation that, at the time, had a population of just under five million. The masses of visitors inside the shrine can be oppressive at times, but is an indication of the continued public interest in the country's war history.

You can head up to the roof if it's too much, and enjoy the fabulous all-round views beyond the tree tops of the *Royal Botanic Gardens. Daily 10am–5pm, guided tours daily 10am, 11am, 1pm, 2pm, 3pm & 4pm | admission free | Kings Domain | Birdwood Av | shrine.org.au | ⏲ 1 hr*

ROYAL BOTANIC GARDENS ★

The botanic garden on the banks of the Yarra covers more than 35,000m² and is the city's green gem, with lakes, foot and cycle paths, more than 60,000 plants from rare species from all over the world, plus parrots, flying foxes, nocturnally active possums,

Venice? Bangkok? Cambridge? Float through Melbourne's Royal Botanic Gardens

shady avenues of trees, sundry theme gardens and elegant tea rooms. In summer, there are open-air performances on the covered *Sidney Myer Music Bowl* stage in the evenings.

The *Aboriginal Heritage Walk (Sun–Fri 11am, duration approx. 90 mins | A$45 | reservations tel. 03 92 52 24 29)* is a special highlight. Koori guides tells visitors of their history and culture on a stroll around the botanic garden. They explain which plants and types of fruit the Aboriginal people gathered for food or medicine and how they prepared them. *Daily 7.30am until dusk | admission free | Visitors Centre/Observatory Gate, Birdwood Av | rbg.vic.gov.au*

INSIDER TIP
Aboriginal Heritage Walk

MELBOURNE MUSEUM ★

The futuristic, interactive museum impressively combines architecture and the natural environment – you can even walk through a wood in the middle of the museum. The *Bunjilaka Aboriginal Cultural Centre* is an excellent introduction to the spiritual, cultural and political history and contemporary life of Victoria's and Australia's First Peoples. *Daily 9am–5pm | A$15 | Nicholson St/Carlton Gardens | museumsvictoria.com.au/melbourne museum | 1½ hrs*

DOCKLANDS

A modern suburb has been created at Victoria Harbour on the western side of the city with upscale architecture in steel and glass. It is as famous for its highly priced apartments as for its popular restaurants, featuring a huge range of world cuisines. Enjoy a glass of wine at a waterside bar, or take a stroll and enjoy the area's public art.

CARLTON

This suburb's Golden Age was during the 1960s, when Italian immigrants showed the Melburnians what real coffee should taste like and proved that spaghetti doesn't have to come in tins. Tiamo and Tiamo 2 are part of this Italian heritage, but they've since been joined by other cuisines – from Moroccan to Japanese – to create a gourmet strip along Lygon Street.

ST KILDA

The best-known suburb near the water is like a socioeconomic résumé of Melbourne. Chic meets shabby, trendy meets retro, elitist meets mainstream. On Acland Street there are designer boutiques next door to second-hand shops, while the fragrance from the vast piles of finest baked goods outside the windows competes with the smell of fish and chips.

Artists and craftspeople offer their wares on the palm-fringed *Esplanade (stkildaesplanademarket.com.au)* on Sundays *(10am–5pm)*. St Kilda Pier, with its extension that opened in 2024, is a real eye-catcher. Stay for an evening meal at the *Little Blue Restaurant (Wed–Mon until 6pm, Thu–Sat until 9pm | littlebluerestaurant.com.au | $$–$$$)*.

Incidentally, behind a kiosk on the pier lives a colony of little penguins.

Hang around St Kilda Beach until sunset – it's worth the wait!

INSIDER TIP
Suburban penguins

At sunset you can watch the penguins waddle down to their burrows under the pier. *short.travel/aus60*

WILLIAMSTOWN

In this nostalgic port district, the modern city of Melbourne seems miles away and yet it is within eyeshot on the far side of Port Philip. Those interested in history and the romantically inclined should definitely pay a visit. The best way to get there is to take the *Williamstown Ferry (daily from Southgate | A$35 | melbcruises.com.au/williamstown-ferry)* across the Yarra River. The 50-minute trip gives you a picture of the old and new dockland areas, and approaching Williamstown by water is how it would have been seen in the early 19th century when people arrived on sailing ships. At that time, the international port was supposed to have been expanded – but then Melbourne grew in importance.

Many historical buildings line Nelson Place: modest houses have been preserved, as have some grander homes, old pubs and imposing civic buildings. These often house small shops or restaurants, which are a welcome stop on any tour.

INSIDER TIP
A stylish swimming spot

Wind down in summer with a swim on *Williamstown Beach*. *visitwilliamstown.com.au*

EATING & DRINKING

COOKIE

A location with fabulous Thai cuisine, a super bar atmosphere and the popular nightclub, *Toff (Tue–Sat | thetoff.com.au)*, on the second floor. Happy hour – weekdays from 4pm to 6pm – offers cocktails for A$12. *Daily | 1st floor, 252 Swanston St, Curtin House | tel. 03 96 63 76 60 | cookie.net.au | $$*

RICHMOND OYSTERS

If you like oysters, then this is the place for you. And if you're not so keen on shellfish, you can order freshly caught fish – in the restaurant or shop. *Closed Sun | 437 Church St | tel. 03 94 28 51 21 | richmondoysters.com.au | $$*

RUYI MODERN CHINESE

Take a few hours to enjoy the individual courses at this Chinese speciality restaurant. Ideally, order the five-course menu (there is also a vegetarian option) with the recommended wines. *Closed Sun/Mon | 16 Liverpool St | tel. 03 90 90 77 78 | ruyi.com.au | $$$*

COLLINGWOOD CHILDREN'S FARM

Every city needs a taste of the country, and city-based nature is certainly a highlight in Melbourne – especially for younger visitors! With meandering meadows and huge, well kept animal enclosures, this picture-book farm will have kids falling in love with country life: think petting goats, watching the cows being milked, helping the gardener and riding ponies. *Daily 9.15am–4.45pm | A$17, children A$8 | 18 St Heliers St, Abbotsford | farm.org.au*

SHOPPING

The perfect route for shopping fans: start on *Flinders Street*, opposite *Flinders Street Station*, and head for *Degraves Street*. Cross *Flinders Lane* and on to *Centre Place* (between *Flinders Lane* and *Collins Street*). Cross over *Collins Street (collinsstreet.com.au)*, Melbourne's most elegant shopping mile, and head for the *Block Arcade*, diagonally opposite. It leads you to *Little Collins Street*, which is especially interesting between the *Block Arcade* and *Russell Street*. Nearby is the Royal Arcade *(Elizabeth St/corner of Bourke Street Mall and Elizabeth St)*, the city's oldest shopping centre.

CHAPEL STREET

Melbourne's famous shopping street stretches from Windsor in the south through handsome Prahran as far as upmarket South Yarra. Take your pick from local and international fashion labels, jewellery shops, book stores and vintage emporia. *chapelstreet.com.au*

MELBOURNE CENTRAL

Shopping centre with some 180 shops, restaurants and boutiques that stock Australian labels such as *RM Williams* (stylish outback fashions). The Central is an architectural work of art: the 50m, brick-built *Shot Tower* (lead shot was produced here between 1888 and 1967) is surrounded by an 84m-high conical glass roof. *Swanston St/La Trobe St | melbournecentral.com.au*

QUEEN VICTORIA MARKET

Little in youthful Melbourne is as well established as "Vic Market". Since the 1870s, half the city has been congregating here at the weekend to fill its storage cupboards. Souvenirs and clothing are also sold. *Tue, Thu/Fri 6am–3pm, Sat 6am–4pm, Sun 9am–4pm | qvm.com.au*

SPORT & ACTIVITIES

BIKE HIRE

Want to explore Melbourne on two wheels? Bicycles (including those with child seats), e-bikes and mountain bikes are available from *Blue Tongue Bikes (from A$30/day | 2 Rebecca Walk, near Southern Cross Station | bluetonguebikes.com.au)*.

STAND-UP PADDLING

Have you always fancied giving SUP a go? There's nowhere better to start than off beautiful St Kilda beach with views of the Melbourne skyline? Beginner lessons start daily at 9am and 10.30am *(A$60)* or you can just rent your own board and paddle *(A$30/hr) Pier Rd, St Kilda West | supb.com.au*

NIGHTLIFE

Ballet, classical music, theatre and opera are the main features on the programme at the *Arts Centre Melbourne (tickets: artscentremelbourne.com.au)*. Every Tuesday at noon, *TIXAT12 (short.travel/aus61)* releases a few discounted tickets for that week's performances.

Melbourne has plenty of variety for night owls. Nightlife hubs include Fitzroy, Northcote and Brunswick. You're more likely to find the alternative scene at venues such as *Bar Open (daily | 317 Brunswick St | baropen.com.au)* and the *Kodiak Club (Wed–Sun | 272 Brunswick St | kodiakclub.com)*. South Yarra, with its trendy bars and nightclubs, is also popular,

Take a break from shopping in the Block Arcade's cafés

especially Chapel Street. To find out what's happening where, go to *beat.com.au* and *timeout.com/melbourne*.

AROUND MELBOURNE

1 PHILLIP ISLAND ★

142km / 2 hrs from Melbourne by car

This island southeast of Melbourne is one of the region's most popular destinations for day trips. This is thanks to the little penguins that come out of the water here in the evenings and leisurely retire to their burrows. You can watch them from designated viewing platforms *(penguins.org.au)*. Tickets *(from A$32)* and times online or from the *Phillip Island Information Centre (109 Ventnor Rd, Summerlands | visitphillipisland.com)*.

Another attraction is *The Nobbies Centre (admission free)*, on the southwest tip, where a boardwalk leads down to the shore. With a little luck you might see some members of Australia's largest seal colony. Boat trips to see the local wildlife are arranged by *Wildlife Coast Cruises (from A$102 | wildlifecoastcruises.com.au)*. G7

INSIDER TIP **Seal-spotting!**

Birdwatching is all part of the Wilsons Promontory experience

2 WILSONS PROMONTORY NATIONAL PARK

225km / 3¼ hrs from Melbourne by car

Wilsons Promontory is in Gippslands, southeast of Melbourne *(on the coast road towards New South Wales)* and offers a paradise for nature-lovers, hikers and wildlife enthusiasts. Wombats feel very much at home here, particularly on *Norman Beach.* The wallabies, possums, emus and koalas that also live here are most active at dusk. Brightly coloured parrots and thousands of waterfowl live in the eucalyptus forests and the swamps of the river estuary, and dolphins, penguins and seals frolic near the white beaches around the peninsula. Here, *Squeaky Beach* is aptly named. No special technique is needed to make the sand squeak under your feet.

INSIDER TIP **Noisy sand**

If you've had enough of beach life, there are lovely trails through the national park. But remember, you'll need to bring food and drink with you. Find maps and trail information at the *Visitor Centre* in Tidal River or online *(short.travel/aus49).* *H7*

3 APOLLO BAY

190km / 3 hrs from Melbourne by car

This pretty fishing village (pop. 1,500) with a beach and a diverse hinterland is perfect for a longish stop along the *Great Ocean Road* (see p. 174). There are plenty of places to stay right by the beautiful beach, while nearby *Barham River Valley* offers excellent hikes, and don't miss the view from *Marriner's Lookout*.

Nearby is *Wildlife Wonders (daily 9.30am–5pm | admission incl. tour A$59 | 475 Great Ocean Rd | wildlifewonders.org.au)* with its curious emus, lazy koalas and dense eucalyptus forest. Here, you can experience the region known as the Otways as it was before human settlement. G7

4 GREAT OTWAY NATIONAL PARK

210km / 3¼ hrs from Melbourne by car

If you're looking for an earthly setting for a fairy tale, these ancient rainforests (to the southwest of the city), with their waterfalls and gigantic eucalyptus trees, are just the place. Trees, ferns and bushes wind around each other in their fight for sunlight. Roots hang from high branches, while koalas slumber in the branch forks.

On the *Otway Fly Treetop Walk (daily 9am–5pm | admission A$28 | Beech Forest | otwayfly.com)*, you walk 25m above the ground among the huge trees. Alternatively, you can unleash your inner Tarzan on the 2½-hour ziplining tour *(A$120)*. If you follow the Lighthouse Road to the lighthouse on the cape, you're more than likely to spot koalas roaming free. G7

INSIDER TIP
Look out for koalas

5 PORT CAMPBELL NATIONAL PARK ★

290km / 4½ hrs from Melbourne by car along the Great Ocean Road

This narrow nature reserve adjacent to the coast west of Melbourne is home to all the highlights that are familiar to you from the tourist brochures. Conveniently, it's all along the *Great Ocean Road* *(see p. 174)*. The *Twelve Apostles* are especially atmospheric early in the morning or in the evening.

For an interesting view of the limestone stacks, go from the car park at Gibson Steps down the steps to the beach. Not quite so well known, but every bit as spectacular, are formations like *The Grotto, Loch Arch Gorge* and the *Bay of Martyrs*. G7

GRAMPIANS

(G7) **Just three hours by car from Melbourne, the sandstone ranges (up to 1,000m) of the ★ Grampians rise up out of the green landscape – a paradise for hikers and nature lovers.**

Brightly coloured parrots screech in the trees, while emus and kangaroos also consider the campsites to be their terrain. And above it all is the glorious deep-blue sky. The mountains, called *Gariwerd* in the local Aboriginal language, are witnesses to an ancient culture: Aboriginal people lived here for 5,000 years before the Europeans came.

A good starting point is the small town of *Halls Gap* at the northeastern

The other-worldly Balconies are a sight to behold in the Grampian Mountains

end of the national park, with a wide range of accommodation, restaurants and a supermarket.

SIGHTSEEING

BRAMBUK ABORIGINAL CULTURAL CENTRE

The Grampians are also known for their Aboriginal culture. The vegetation here was so plentiful that local Indigenous groups had time for artistic and religious pursuits alongside hunting and gathering food. It's no coincidence that the Grampians are home to about 80 per cent of all known Aboriginal rock paintings in Victoria. The imposing cultural centre here holds exhibitions and events to promote this heritage, and the complex also includes the *Gariwerd Dreaming Theatre*, where two short documentaries on local Aboriginal culture are shown. *Daily 9am–5pm | admission free | 277 Grampians Rd, Halls Gap | short.travel/aus53 | 1 hr*

EATING & DRINKING

It can get busy here at weekends in the summer, so it's always best to book.

SPIRIT OF PUNJAB

Excellent Indian dishes are served here, many of which are vegetarian. Plus you get to decide how brave – read spicy – you're feeling. *Daily | 161 Grampians Rd, Halls Gap | tel. 03 53 56 42 34 | spiritofpunjab restaurant.com | $$*

KOOKABURRA HOTEL

There's something for everyone here, whether that be pub classics like fish and chips, or beef tenderloin, kangaroo fillet or a spinach crêpe. *Tue–Sun 5.30–8.30pm, Sat/Sun noon–3pm | 125 Grampians Rd, Halls Gap | tel. 03 53 56 42 22 | kookaburrahotel.com.au | $$*

SPORT & ACTIVITIES

There are more than enough hiking trails and mountain bike tracks here. If you want something quick and easy, then try the much-photographed *Balconies* rock formation. The 90-minute (round trip) hike from Wonderland car park to *Pinnacle Lookout* is more challenging, but you'll be rewarded with sensational views – plus the last stretch takes you through a narrow crevice in the rock.

INSIDER TIP
Rocky routes, fabulous views

The thundering *MacKenzie Falls* has its charms, but that's common knowledge. For a less crowded option, try the *Beehive Falls*, which can be reached in about 30 minutes from the car park of the same name.

SLEEP WELL IN VICTORIA

DON'T CAMP, GLAMP!

Do you love the wilderness but miss the comforts of home? Try one of the glamping tents at ⚑ *Wilderness Retreats (32 Ring Rd | tel. 03 84 27 21 22 | wildernessretreats.com.au | $$$)* near Tidal River in Wilsons Promontory National Park. Make sure to book early as the four permanent tents complete with heating and right at the heart of the national park are snapped up quickly!

CABINS & KANGAROOS

You'll sleep very well in one of the 25 comfortable log cabins with verandas and fabulous mountain views at the adults-only *D'Altons Resort (Glen St, Halls Gap | tel. 03 53 56 46 66 | daltonsstudios.com.au | $$)* in the Grampians. Plus, there are animal guests too: every evening, the kangaroos hop into the large garden in search of food – totally unfazed by open-mouthed human visitors.

QUEENSLAND

THE RADIANT SUNSHINE STATE

Snorkelling mask on and let's go! Soft corals sway in the current while a clownfish grazes on some algae. Wait, was that a shark back there?

The ★ *Great Barrier Reef*, with its fascinating undersea world, runs for more than 2,300km up the east coast of Australia from Lady Elliot Island to the northernmost tip of Cape York; Queensland's main attraction comprises more than 3,000 individual reefs and over 2,000 tropical islands. But Queensland has much more to offer.

On Mission Beach the rainforest reaches right up to the edge of the sand

It's not known as the "Sunshine State" for nothing. Its vibrant capital, Brisbane, boasts over 300 sunshine days per year; the beaches of the Gold Coast and Sunshine Coast offer the finest surf and sand, while the wonders of the outback can be discovered in the interior – from dinosaur footprints to Aboriginal dance festivals.

Queensland is the second largest state in Australia, covering 1.7 million km² (almost seven times the size of the UK), but it has a population of less than six million.

QUEENSLAND

MARCO POLO BUCKET LIST

3 ✓ Marvel at the reef

Learn how tourism can help protect nature on a boat trip to the *Great Barrier Reef* ➤ p. 99

4 ✓ Go for a walk with a local guide

Listen well: the rainforest in the *Mossman Gorge* is full of spirits and stories ➤ p. 106

MARCO POLO HIGHLIGHTS

★ GREAT BARRIER REEF
The attraction par excellence on the east coast: millions of brightly coloured fish, dolphins, corals and tropical islands ➤ p. 88

★ BRISBANE
Pubs with music, world-class restaurants and up-and-coming art – it's all here without any of that big-city hustle and bustle ➤ p. 92

★ K'GARI (FRASER ISLAND)
Whales and dolphins swim in the unbelievably blue waters, while dingoes roam the jungle of this huge sand island ➤ p. 96

★ WHITSUNDAY ISLANDS
Nowhere is the sand whiter, the ocean bluer or the cocktail in your hand more refreshing ➤ p. 98

★ SKYRAIL
Glide in a cabin over gorges above the rainforest canopy ➤ p. 102

★ DAINTREE NATIONAL PARK
Tropical rainforests, dream-like beaches and cloud-covered mountains ➤ p. 106

BRISBANE

(🕮 J5) ★ **Brisbane is like a year-round summer fairy tale: it's almost always T-shirt weather; children splash around in the artificial lagoon, and in the cooler evening hours local bands rock the scene on the rooftop terraces.**

It's hard to imagine that the metropolis owes its existence to a few Conservative British politicians in the early 19th century, who strongly disagreed with liberalisation in New South Wales. They wanted to reinforce transportation to Australia as a "measure of sheer terror" by opening a new penal colony in Moreton Bay. This situation didn't last long, though, and after less than 20 years, the colony was dissolved and Brisbane quickly grew to become a thriving centre, not least thanks to gold being found here in the 20th century.

WHERE TO START?

You can find your way about this city quickly. The real centre is **King George Square**: walk a few yards to **Queen Street Mall** and then on to the **Brisbane River**. Cross Victoria Bridge and stroll through the idyllic South Bank Parklands. If you arrive by train, get off at **Roma Street Station**. Buses from all directions stop in the centre. For drivers, multistorey car parks can be found in the **Myer Centre**, among other places.

With a population of 2.7 million, Brisbane is now the third-biggest city in Australia. Despite that, though, apart from at rush hour, it has little of the usual city hustle and bustle.

Queensland's capital not only produces talented musicians – think the Bee Gees and Savage Garden – but also has an excellent pub and restaurant scene. *visit.brisbane.qld.au*

SIGHTSEEING

QUEENSLAND CULTURAL CENTRE

The colossal concrete complex on the south bank of the river and on both sides of Victoria Bridge in the South Bank Parklands cannot fail to impress with its gallery, museum, library and theatre. The *Queensland Art Gallery (daily 10am–5pm | admission free, excluding special exhibitions | qagoma.qld.gov.au)*, puts on high-quality temporary exhibitions of Aboriginal art and European painting and sculpture. Together with the *Gallery of Modern Art (GoMA)* it is the largest modern art gallery in Australia. The *Queensland Museum (daily 9.30am–5pm | admission free | qm.qld.gov.au)* has rich displays on the history and natural history of Queensland. *arts.qld.gov.au/arts/culturalcentre | ⏲ 1–1½ hrs each*

SOUTH BANK PARKLANDS

An Australian metropolis without access to the sea – is there any such thing? Yes – but to make up for it, Brisbane simply brought the beach into the city. You can relax on the man-made *Streets Beach* beside the

tropical lagoon, or go for a stroll along the *Arbour Path*, which is flanked by brightly coloured flowers – all with views of the city skyline. The view from above is courtesy of the *Wheel of Brisbane (Sun–Thu 10am–10pm, Fri, Sat until 11pm | A$21 | thewheelof brisbane.com.au)*. There are many restaurants and food stalls in the vicinity, and you can stroll around a weekend market selling everything from art to gifts and vintage clothing. *visitsouthbank.com.au*

LONE PINE KOALA SANCTUARY

No visit to Australia is complete until you have cuddled a koala. And where better to do that than at the world's biggest koala sanctuary? This idyllic animal park, which is also home to kangaroos, Tasmanian devils and other Australian animals, supports numerous animal welfare projects. *Daily 9am–5pm | A$39 | Fig Tree Pocket, Jesmond Rd | lonepinekoala sanctuary.com | ⏲ 2 hrs*

EATING & DRINKING

Excellent restaurants are to be found at the *Riverside Centre* and *Eagle Street Pier* as well as *Fortitude Valley* and in *New Farm (Merthyr Rd/ Brunswick St)*. *Given Terrace* and *Caxton Street (Paddington)* as well as *Park Road (Milton)* are further recommendations, as is *South Bank*.

ALCHEMY RESTAURANT & BAR

Located on the riverfront, this contemporary restaurant serves top-quality dishes against the backdrop of Story Bridge and the Brisbane River. *Tue, Thu, Fri noon–3pm, 5.30–11pm; Wed noon–2pm, 5.30–11pm; Sat 5.30pm–late | 175 Eagle Street | tel. 07 32 29 31 75 | alchemyrestaurant.com.au | $$$*

BREAKFAST CREEK HOTEL

This old building, not unlike a country house, is home to a Queensland institution. Excellent beers and the best steaks in the city are served in several bars and restaurants, as well as at what is said to be Brisbane's oldest beer garden. *Daily | 2 Kingsford Smith Drive | tel. 02 32 62 59 88 | breakfast creekhotel.com | $$$*

SHOPPING

The main shopping drag is *Queen Street Mall* with the pleasant *Brisbane Arcade*. Pop in and have a look at *Maiocchi (maiocchi.com.au)* – for racks and racks of chic, Australian-designed and made ladies' fashion. *Riverside Market (Sun 8am–3pm, Botanical Garden)* is worth visiting too.

NIGHTLIFE

A number of good bars and nightclubs can be found in *Fortitude Valley* on *Ann Street*, e.g. *Beat Mega Club (No. 677)* and *GPO Hotel (No. 740)*. Perhaps unsurprisingly in the home of some of Australia's best bands, great live music is also played at, for example, *Tivoli (open for events | 52 Costin St)*. You'll also find good vibes and good music at the *Sound Garden (Wed–Fri from 11am, Sat from 3pm, Sun from 5pm | 312–318 Brunswick St | thesoundgarden.com.au)*.

Value-added shopping: the 100-year-old Brisbane Arcade is full of atmosphere

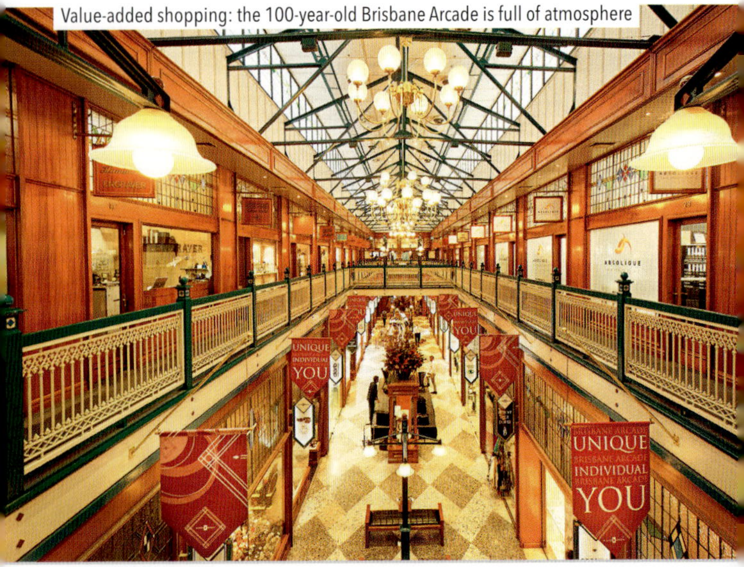

AROUND BRISBANE

1 NORTH STRADBROKE ISLAND

45km / 1½ hrs from Brisbane by car and ferry

You've probably heard of K'gari (Fraser Island), but what about North Stradbroke? "Straddie" is the world's second-largest sand island, where everything, just like on Fraser Island, grows on sand. If you don't believe us, take a look at the idyllic eucalyptus forests complete with koalas taking a nap in their branch forks! Over in the small town of *Point Lookout*, the name says it all, with incredible ocean views wherever you look. Restaurants, bakeries and a supermarket line the main street.

INSIDER TIP Go walkabout

No trip is complete without a walk to Headland Park at the end of this road – the start of two first-class short walks: the *North* and *South Gorge Walks*. The two walks merge into one another, and you can quite easily walk them in half an hour *(one way)*. But it's worth leaving more time because kangaroos often jump out on the path – and anyway, this is a view to be savoured. You can spot a whale a minute (almost literally) off the coast during whale season, and the dolphins and manta rays are an added bonus. Take the *car ferry* to the island *(car incl. 2 adults from A$100 | sealink.com.au)* from Cleveland. *stradbrokeisland.com* | *J5*

2 GOLD COAST

78km / 1 hr from Brisbane by car

Hardly any other strip of sand is more of an Australian holiday cliché than this. There are no limits to the pleasure available on the narrow, approximately 70km-long coastal strip: high-rise luxury hotels, modern apartment blocks, nightclubs, huge shopping malls and casinos compete for the favours of the millions of visitors who come here every year. The centre is *Surfers Paradise*, a mass of concrete and neon that is not unlike Las Vegas. There are several first-class theme parks in the surrounding area, which you can see in the distance from the *SkyPoint Observation Deck* on the 77th floor of the Q1 Skyscraper *(daily 7.30am–9pm | A$28 | Hamilton Av | skypoint.com.au)*. Further information at *destinationgoldcoast.com*. *J5*

3 LAMINGTON NATIONAL PARK

106km / 1½ hrs from Brisbane by car

Inland from the Gold Coast, this network of paths covering 160km runs through the hilly countryside of the McPherson Range. *O'Reilly's Rainforest Retreat (Lamington National Park Rd, via Canungra | oreillys.com.au)* organises excellent guided hikes through the rainforest. The 800m *Tree Top Walk* takes you over nine swinging suspension bridges through the rainforest before you get to enjoy the view out over the national park from *Mick's Tower*, 18m above the ground. *F5*

4 SUNSHINE COAST

135km / 1¾ hrs from Brisbane by car

It does what it says on the tin: dreamy beaches, like the 150km stretch between Bribie Island and Fraser Island, and pretty resorts. And the sun does almost always shine.

The trip from *Caloundra* to *Noosa Heads (noosaeguide.com)* in the north is very worthwhile. This lovely spot, together with the adjoining town of *Noosaville*, is the touristic heart of the Sunshine Coast *(visitsunshinecoast.com)*. During the day, people go to the wonderfully wide sheltered beaches such as *Main Beach, Marcus Beach or Peregian Beach*. Evenings can be spent in the many street cafés and restaurants on Hastings Street. Later you can promenade along the boardwalk under a wide starry sky. You can go for a short walk in the small *Noosa National Park* close to the city that covers an area of just 4.3km². Remember to look up: there are koalas around.

The rugged sandstone cliff landscape in *Cooloola National Park* to the north can only be explored in a 4WD vehicle, or on a tour, like the one organised by *Great Beach Drive (day tour from A$215 | greatbeachdrive-4wdtours.com)*. For cheaper transport links from Brisbane try *Col's Airshuttle (tel. 07 54 50 59 33 | airshuttle.com.au)*. *J5*

5 FRASER COAST

386km / 3½ hrs from Brisbane by car

The Fraser Coast, almost 400km north of Brisbane, is well known for two reasons. *Hervey Bay* (pronounced "Harvey") is considered by experts to be an excellent place for whale watching. Between August and October there are countless humpback whales in the waters off the city. A number of different tours start from *Urangan Boat Harbour*. Information: *Hervey Bay Tourism (Urraween Rd/Maryborough Rd | discoverherveybay.com, visitfrasercoast.com)*.

★ *K'gari (Fraser Island)* is also unique in the world: covering 1,840km², it is the largest sand island on earth and became a UNESCO World Heritage Site in 1992. The island is up to 240m high and home to an extraordinary variety of plants and animals. The rainforests and some 40 freshwater lakes can be reached along a sandy track. One of the most beautiful lakes, with a snow-white beach, is *Lake McKenzie*. The island's east coast is the busiest, and the beach can turn into a bit of a motorway. If you've got a little more time, and some off-road driving experience, venture up to the north-west coast of the island, where an almost untouched natural paradise awaits. *K'gari* – since 2021 the island has officially borne its original name – can be explored on a well-guided tour or in your own all-terrain vehicle *(permission required | short.travel/aus39)*. You can get to the island paradise from Hervey Beach by charter aircraft or ferry.

INSIDER TIP **Solitude in the sand**

Ferries also go to Fraser Island from *Rainbow Beach* further south, which has idyllic sand dunes and is much quieter and more relaxed. *J4*

Destination dream beach: you'll need an all-terrain vehicle to travel on K'gari

AIRLIE BEACH

(◫ 113) **The small, lively holiday resort of Airlie Beach (pop. 8,000) is the gateway to the Whitsunday Islands.**

By day, wearing your diving kit or snorkelling goggles, you can jump from the tour boat to explore the colourful world of the coral reefs, or lie back and enjoy the feeling of the sun on your body as you relax in "Airlie's" artificial lagoon. Come the evening, join the "in" crowd and party outdoors at the clubs and pubs on the town's only main street, *Airlie Beach Road.*

EATING & DRINKING

WHITSUNDAY SAILING CLUB

Meet the locals! There are fabulous views of the sea from the large terrace, the food is reliably good and portions generous. *Daily | Airlie Point | tel. 07 49 46 61 38 | $$*

SPORT & ACTIVITIES

CRUISE WHITSUNDAYS

Cruise Whitsundays ferries take you from Airlie Beach to Daydream Island (overnight stay required) and Hamilton Island. There are also organised day trips to the reef with time to snorkel or trips to various islands, such as Whitsunday Island. *Port of Airlie | tel. 07 48 46 70 00 | cruisewhitsundays.com*

Snorkelling is an easy way to experience the colourful underwater world

FLIGHTS OVER THE REEF

Admire the Great Barrier Reef from the air and from the water: after an airborne tour, the Air Whitsunday amphibious aircraft lands directly on the reef and releases its passengers for some snorkelling. *A$700 | tel. 07 49 46 46 71 | airwhitsunday.com.au | 4½ hrs*

DIVING

Many diving schools offer trips and courses over a few days for beginners and experienced divers, for example *Whitsunday Scuba Centre (tours with dive from A$350 | 1/4 Airlie Esplanade | tel. 07 49 48 12 39 | whitsundaydivecentre.com.au).*

AROUND AIRLIE BEACH

Off the coast around Airlie Beach are the 74 tropical islands that make up the ★ *Whitsunday Islands (H3)*. Only eight of them are inhabited. Some are purely holiday islands with hotel complexes and nightlife, others are protected national parks that can be visited on day trips. Excursion boats can drop the romantically inclined and adventurous off for a night or a few days on some of the many uninhabited islands, such as *Whitsunday*

Island. This island is a particularly attractive national park with mangrove swamps and the snow-white, fine-sandy *Whitehaven Beach*, the most beautiful beach in Queensland. *Hook Island, Long Island, South Molle Island* and *Whitsunday Island* all have campsites where you can stay overnight with a *camping permit*. For useful information and accommodation and tour options go to *tourismwhitsundays.com*

6 DAYDREAM ISLAND

5km / ½ hr from Airlie Beach by ferry

This island seems to have been cut straight out of a catalogue of dream destinations: white coral beaches with palms waving in the breeze behind them, with flower-filled gardens further inland below rainforest-clad slopes. The privately owned island is currently only accessible to guests of the resort *(daydreamisland.com)*. Here you can relax on your lounger by the pool under palm trees, eating shrimp and drinking cocktails – welcome to paradise. *H3*

7 HAMILTON ISLAND

20km / 1 hr from Airlie Beach by ferry

The biggest inhabited Whitsunday island also has the best tourist infrastructure – with all the associated advantages and disadvantages. Qantas, Jetstar and Virgin Australia fly direct to the island from Melbourne,

SUICIDE ON THE REEF

Day after day, countless boats bring tourists to the beautiful diving and snorkelling areas of the Great Barrier Reef. The question is, for how much longer?

Rising water temperatures are causing difficulties for the corals, which are slowly but surely releasing a deadly stress reaction. The colourful algae that live on the corals and are responsible for the stunning colours are being rejected by their hosts. It is effectively suicide, because the corals will not be able to survive without the algae.

Mass coral bleaching events occurred on the reef in 2016, 2017, 2020, 2022 and 2024. Because of this, the reef could soon be placed on the IUCN (International Union for Conservation of Nature) Red List of Threatened Species.

Nevertheless, tourism is important, as thanks to tours of the reef, developments are documented, illegal fishing is curbed and every visitor pays a reef tax. Many tour boats also carry Master Reef Guides who provide information about conservation projects. If you'd like to do your own research, further information is available from the *Marine Environment Protection Authority (qld.gov.au/en/vironment)*. You can also participate in projects like *Eye on the Reef (www2.gbrmpa.gov.au)* or the *Marine Discovery Program (marinediscoveries.com.au)*.

Day-trippers miss the idyllic evening atmosphere on Magnetic Island

Brisbane, Cairns and Sydney. Although the various hotels do cause noticeably more traffic on the beaches, this does not detract from their beauty. There are regular ferries from Hamilton to Airlie Beach, or you can join a day-trip to the reef or Whitehaven Beach. *hamiltonisland.com.au.* *(🕮 H3)*

TOWNSVILLE

(🕮 H3) **You might not instantly be bowled over by this busy harbour town (pop. 234,000) halfway between Airlie Beach and Cairns.**

But don't reject it too hastily, because the attractive promenade *The Strand,* with lots of restaurants and beach sections (with jellyfish nets), is perfect for relaxing. From the granite rock *Castle Hill* you can see all the way to interesting Magnetic Island, which is well worth a visit

SIGHTSEEING

GREAT BARRIER REEF AQUARIUM

The huge aquarium, which is dedicated to research into the Great Barrier Reef, will reopen after renovations in 2026. *2 Flinders St | greatbarrierreef aquarium.au*

EATING & DRINKING

THE WATERMARK

Café and restaurant with a trendy, cool design and modern Australian cuisine, with views over Strand Park to the sea. *Daily | 72 The Strand | tel. 07 47 72 42 81 | watermarktownsville.com.au | $$*

AROUND TOWNSVILLE

8 MAGNETIC ISLAND

8km / 25 mins from Townsville by ferry

This holiday island with lovely beaches and a much slower pace is a popular destination for day trippers. Drive to pretty Horseshoe Bay to the north of the island, where a jellyfish net guarantees safe bathing. Ferries depart from Breakwater Terminal: *Sealink (return approx. A$38 | sealink.com.au). visitmagneticisland.com.au | (🕮 H3)*

9 MUSEUM OF UNDERWATER ART

80km from Townsville by boat

Ocean Sentinels is an art installation by the underwater sculptor Jason deCaires Taylor. The figurative statues are located on the seabed off the coast of Townsville at a depth of 16m to 18m, alongside wooden sculptures and a coral nursery, all of which contribute to the regeneration of the reef. Snorkelling will give you an impression of the installation, but only divers will get the full effect. Day-trips to the site are offered by *Adrenaline Dive & Snorkel (from A$354 | adrenalindive.com.au). 🕮 H3*

CAIRNS

(🕮 H2) **The picturesque northern town of Cairns (pop. 254,000) is the perfect starting point for boat trips to the Great Barrier Reef, hikes through the tropical rainforest and excursions to Australia's northernmost point, Cape York.**

It's instantly obvious that Cairns lives and breathes mass tourism. But with the world's biggest coral reef right at the front door, the brightly coloured underwater world of the Great Barrier Reef, that's no surpise. Cairns is at its busiest on the picturesque *Esplanade*, where you can cool down in the man-made bathing lagoon, enjoy a huge ice cream and browse the various souvenir shops. And when the sun sinks behind the tableland, the numerous pubs and restaurants come to life. There's also always something going on along the beach promenade, where information panels impart the city's history as you walk by.

WHERE TO START?

The **esplanade** in the city centre is bursting with life. You'll find all sorts of eateries, hotels, the lagoon for an inviting swim and streets of shops around the corner. The harbour with boat tours to the Great Barrier Reef is just a short walk away. From the railway station it's about 15 minutes on foot; from the airport just a 10-minute drive by taxi or shuttle bus.

Grab dinner at Cairns' Night Market before you do some shopping

SIGHTSEEING

CAIRNS MUSEUM

Cairns has a rather unusual history. In just two centuries, a once-pristine coastline transformed into a coveted gold rush hotspot and then tourist magnet. Travel through the city's history for yourself here in the museum. *Mon–Sat 10am–4pm | A$15 | Lake St, corner of Shields St | cairnsmuseum.org.au | 1 hr*

CAIRNS AQUARIUM

A reef you can walk through. The aquarium offers young and old alike a bright and fun learning environment dedicated to the reef and the tropics. Make sure you check the programme online before you go so you don't miss the presentation every half hour. *Daily 9am–5pm | A$61, children A$35 | Lake St, corner of Florence St | cairnsaquarium.com.au | 2 hrs*

FLECKER BOTANIC GARDENS

Immerse yourself in the rich variety of tropical plants with a visit to this garden, home to more than 100 different species of palm tree, orchids and climbers. At the *Aboriginal Plant Use Garden*, you can learn about plants that Indigenous Australians grew thousands of years ago for food or medicine. The gardens are so vast that you can easily spend a whole morning here. *Daily 7.30am–5.30pm | admission free | Collins Av*

SKYRAIL ★

The 7.5km-long cable car takes you into the mountainous countryside inland from Cairns, with its fascinating vegetation. The cabins glide over the valleys and provide views of the waterfalls on *Barron River* too. Explanations on the flora and fauna of the rainforest can be found at two stopping points where you can break your trip en route. The destination is *Kuranda*, once an alternative lifestyle hippie settlement, now a teeming souvenir market. The best way to return is on the *Kuranda Scenic Railway (ksr.com.au)* that makes an adventurous and twisty descent back down to the plain. *Round trip A$135 | from Smithfield Terminal | skyrail.com.au*

EATING & DRINKING

OCHRE RESTAURANT

Aboriginal recipes and ingredients are the attraction at this unusual restaurant. *Daily | 6/1 Marlin Parade | tel. 07 40 51 01 00 | ochrerestaurant.com.au | $$$*

SHOPPING

You'll find souvenirs at the *Night Market* held every evening on the esplanade, and mainly Asian food to quell your hunger. Don't miss the colourful *Rusty's Market (Fri/Sat until 4pm, Sun until 3pm | Grafton St)*, where you can work your way through the variety of exotic fruit.

SPORT & ACTIVITIES

DIVING

Passions of Paradise (tour A$260, diving A$75 | tel. 07 40 42 26 00 | passions.com.au) organises tours for divers and snorkellers to the Outer Reef with marine biologists on board.

ESPLANADE SWIMMING LAGOON

Just a few yards from the town centre you can cool off in this well-cared-for bathing area with a view of the

HOW IT ALL BEGAN

Indigenous Australians believe themselves to be the descendants of primeval ancestral beings. These spirits roamed the once-barren land and created everything that now exists on the planet: water and land, mountains and deserts, plants, animals and people. After their work was complete, the ancestral beings lay down on the ground to sleep, where they remain to this day, in the form of rocks, for example. Their locations are sacred to Aboriginal and Torres Strait Islander people and, in many cases, can only be visited by certain groups. The spirits of the ancestors also live on in totemic forms, such as snakes, sharks and kangaroos.

The creation story has been passed down the centuries as an oral tradition; it not only describes the foundation of the world but also conveys important rules of conduct and offers guidance for Indigenous peoples living in the here and now.

ocean – and it's free! Come early in the afternoon to secure one of the barbecue spots on the grass for a grill party.

EXCURSIONS & CRUISES TO THE REEF

Day trips are organised from Cairns to the Outer Reef *(from A$285)*, e.g. by *Sunlover Reef Cruises (tel. 07 40 50 13 33 | sunlover.com.au)* or a visit to the small coral Green Island by *Great Adventures (tel. 07 40 44 99 44 | greatadventures.com.au)*. You'll be able to snorkel on either tour, but if you want to dive, then take the tour to the Outer Reef.

HELICOPTER FLIGHT

What a treat: a scenic helicopter tour of the Great Barrier Reef with fabulous views and opportunities to take unbeatable photos and videos from the air. Flights last 30, 45 or 60 minutes and cost from A$415 per person with *Nautilus Aviation (nautilus aviation.com.au)*.

AROUND CAIRNS

10 MISSION BEACH

129km / 2 hrs from Cairns by car

As beach holidays north of Cairns have become very expensive, places such as Mission Beach are popular, especially among the younger crowd. The small town is a good place to start a hiking or diving tour *(barrierreef australia.com)*. Day trips to *Dunk Island (greatbarrierreef.org/islands/dunk-island.com)* are also possible. Covered in rainforest, it also has a camping site and café. Just 50km north of Mission Beach, check out *Paronella Park (daily 9am–7.30pm | A$57 | Mena Creek | paronellapark.com.au)*, where a hopeless romantic has built a fairy-tale castle in the tropical parkland. *missionbeachtourism.com.* *🕮 H2*

11 ATHERTON TABLELANDS

68km / 1¼ hrs from Cairns by car

Mountains of volcanic origin covered with dense vegetation tower up to 900m in the uplands west of Cairns. Fascinating ecological niches have evolved in ancient craters, around deep lakes and spectacular waterfalls, and are home to a host of tropical birds and rare animals. One of the loveliest spots is the enigmatic *Mount Hypipamee*, the geological origins of which have yet to be explained. There are wonderful waterfalls with crystal-clear waterholes everywhere in the Tablelands. Four of the most beautiful can be reached on the 15km *Waterfall Circuit* from *Millaa Millaa*. Don't forget your togs!

The little historical town *Yungaburra* (pop. 1,300), which is largely a conservation area, is a great place to start. There are several good restaurants in Yungaburra, such as *Nick's Swiss-Italian Restaurant (Wed–Sat 5–8.30pm, Sun 4–8pm | 33 Gillies Highway | tel. 07 40 95 35 77 | nicksrestaurant.com.au | $$)*, and also antique shops. An authentic market is held in the town every fourth Saturday of the month. *athertontableland.scom.au.* *🕮 H2*

Take a shower under a waterfall in the Atherton Tablelands

12 PALM COVE

30km / ½ hr from Cairns by car

Of all the beach sections to the north of Cairns, Palm Cove is without doubt the most elegant. Luxury resort hotels, cafés and restaurants line the 1.5km-long promenade next to the pristine palm beach. A net in front of the beach protects visitors from jellyfish, meaning a swim is on the cards. Fun fact: The striking, thick-stemmed melaleuca trees along the road are strictly protected and may only be pruned by the authorities, even on private property. Furthermore, no building can be taller than the nearest melaleuca tree! *H2*

INSIDER TIP **Sting-free swimming**

13 PORT DOUGLAS

68km / 1 hr from Cairns by car

The *Captain Cook Highway* is a superb panoramic route running along the coast to Port Douglas (pop. 5,600), 70km north of Cairns. Until the end of the 1980s, this was a modest little village; it has now been transformed into a fashionable holiday resort with generally excellent hotels and restaurants that charge correspondingly high prices *(tourismportdouglas.com.au | visitportdouglasdaintree.com.au).*

Four Mile Beach is an immaculate stretch of beach that starts at the end of *Macrossan Street*, the main road of shops. Climb the stairs at the south-eastern end to reach the lookout point

Rock art tours in the company of a Nugal-warra Elder are available from Cooktown

– we promise the view is worth every bead of sweat! Every morning, at least a dozen sailing boats and catamarans set off for the Great Barrier Reef. Boats operated *by Quicksilver (from A$335 | tel. 07 40 87 21 00 | quicksilver-cruises.com)* moor about 90 minutes later at a pontoon on the Outer Reef, from where diving and snorkelling tours start. *H2*

14 DAINTREE NATIONAL PARK ★

141km / 2¾ hrs from Cairns by car

The protests of committed environmentalists have resulted in Australia's most important and beautiful tropical rainforest being saved from the axe. Today, the breathtaking Daintree National Park, north of Cairns, is a protected area and a UNESCO World Heritage Site. Ancient giant trees, lianas, ferns, palms and moss give way to mangrove forests near the sea. One of the world's largest birds, the flightless cassowary, lives in this fantastic wilderness. Sadly, sightings in the wild are rare as this bird is as shy as it is incredibly fast. Saltwater crocodiles can be seen in the two largest rivers in the national park.

Boat trips on the *Daintree River*, ✓ hikes in the *Mossman Gorge (best with a local guide | A$95/1½ hrs | mossmangorge.com.au)* and at dreamlike *Cape Tribulation* give a good impression of the fragile beauty of this tropical landscape. The road is surfaced as far as Cape Tribulation (a worthwhile destination for a day tour from Cairns or Port Douglas). However, it is narrow in places and leads through the middle of the rainforest.

Daintree is of great spiritual significance to the local Kuku Yalanji people.

INSIDER TIP
Traditional fishing

Along the *Bama Way* between the Daintree River and Cooktown, local people let you gain an insight into their everyday life by joining an Aboriginal fishing expedition, for example. A range of interesting one- to two-day tours is available (*Down Under Tours | tel. 07 40 47 90 97 | downundertours.com*). *H2*

15 CAPE YORK

817km / 18 hrs from Cairns by car

Cape York is a destination for those with a real thirst for adventure. The northernmost point in Australia, enclosed on three sides by the sea, is larger than England but home to only about 10,000 inhabitants, most of whom live in their own territorial areas or settlements. Large areas of Cape York remain unexplored. There are areas of savanna with termite hills several feet high, light-filled eucalyptus forests and rainforest with prolific vegetation.

One solitary road leads from Cairns to the end of the continent, known as *The Tip* or *Pajinka*. The 974km-long stretch is largely a dust track and only drivable in the dry season between May and October. Petrol and simple places to stay can be found in roadhouses or stations along the route.

You should plan five or six days for the one-way route. Guided trips are offered by tour operators in Cairns, including *Heritage Tours (e.g. 7 days' camping with a return flight to Cairns A$4,375 | heritagetours.com.au)*. *G1*

SLEEP WELL IN QUEENSLAND

LUXURY IN THE WILD

Kingfisher Bay Resort (262 rooms | tel. 07 41 20 33 33 | kingfisherbay.com | $$$) on K'gari's west coast is so much more than just a place to rest your head. The huge resort complete with pool blends so idyllically into the landscape you'll start to feel like part of nature yourself.

REST & ADVENTURE

Make yourself at home at eco-registered *On the Wallaby Eco Lodge (38 bed | 34 Eacham Rd, Yungaburra | tel. 07 40 95 20 31 | onthewallaby.com | $)* in the comfortable dormitory or in a good-value double room. Then join a lodge-run tour of the Atherton Tablelands.

NORTHERN TERRITORY

DEEP IN THE WILDERNESS

When you hear the name "Australia", do you yearn for vast and dramatic landscapes, rich in ancient cultures and traditions? If so, then the Northern Territory is the place for you.

You'll gain deep insights into humanity's oldest culture in the fabulous national parks of the tropical north, such as Kakadu and Litchfield. Some of the world's oldest rock paintings are tucked away here too. South of Alice Springs, Uluru – a sacred place for the

Kings Canyon is the main attraction in Watarrka National Park

people of this region – rises up out of the never-ending desert, exerting a mystic pull for tourists from all over the world.

Meanwhile, the other attractions of the Red Centre, such as the rugged mountain chain of the MacDonnell Ranges, impressive Kings Canyon and the unmistakeable rocks of Kata Tjuta, are all worth the long journey.

NORTHERN TERRITORY

MARCO POLO HIGHLIGHTS

★ **LITCHFIELD NATIONAL PARK**
Croc-free swimming in picture-perfect natural pools at the heart of the rainforest ➤ p. 115

★ **KAKADU NATIONAL PARK**
Crocodiles, termite mounds and encounters with mankind's oldest culture ➤ p. 116

★ **NITMILUK (KATHERINE GORGE)**
Canoe your way through the breathtaking gorge ➤ p. 118

★ **KINGS CANYON (WATARRKA)**
Hike through a million-year-old gorge ➤ p. 121

★ **ULURU-KATA TJUTA NATIONAL PARK**
A red monolith and 36 mysterious "heads" ➤ p. 121

MARCO POLO BUCKET LIST

5 ✓ Gaze at a gorgeous panorama
The ascent is steep, but it's the view that will take your breath away on a tour of *Kings Canyon* ➤ p. 121

6 ✓ Be spellbound by a lightshow
Illuminated and choreographed drones tell an ancient Anangu story in the skies above *Uluru* ➤ p. 122

3 Tiwi Islands
155km, 1¾ hrs
Milingimbi
Nhulunbuy
Darwin
p. 112
Jabiru
1 Territory Wildlife Park
Arnhem Land 4
Batchelor
Kakadu National Park ★
p. 116
2 Litchfield National Park ★
Bulman
Alyangula
1
Pine Creek
5 Nitmiluk National Park
24
Katherine
p. 118
Nitmiluk (Katherine Gorge) ★
20
Ngukurr
In the dry season you won't need an off-road all-terrain vehicle to reach most of the destinations within Kakadu National Park.
1
Stuart Hwy
80
1
1210km, 13½ hrs
96
Daguragu
Elliott
Fill up your fuel tank more often than usual when you're travelling along the Stuart Highway. There are long distances between fuel stations and sometimes one of them is unexpectedly closed.
87
NORTHERN TERRITORY
Tennant Creek
66
Canteen Creek
If you're attempting one of the longer hikes, such as the Rim Walk (Watarrka) or the Valley of the Winds Walk (Kata Tjuta), start shortly before dawn and watch how the moon fades in the first rays of sun.
Willowra
A day trip is sufficient for visiting the gorges in the East MacDonnell Ranges. But for the West MacDonnell Ranges you should spend at least one night under canvas or in your camper van.
5
Haasts Bluff
Alice Springs
p. 119
5
Hermannsburg 6
7 Kings Canyon (Watarrka) ★
87
450km, 5¼ hrs
6
Yulara
8 Uluru-Kata Tjuta National Park ★
200 km
124 mi

DARWIN

(▯ D1) **For a long time, it was said that only those fond of digesting flies and chugging pints of beer could find a home in the capital city of the Northern Territory.**

In fact, Darwin (pop. 140,000) has long since brushed off the desert dust to welcome visitors who come to explore its impressive and inviting harbour district, large well-maintained parks and remarkable gastronomy. Try out the food at the waterfront or, even better, at Mindil Beach Sunset Market. The weather, however, is not to everyone's taste: it's either hot and bone dry (May–October) or hot and sticky (the rest of the year).

In any case, most people don't choose Darwin for Darwin itself, but as a base to explore the splendour of the surrounding national parks: Litchfield first and foremast and then, of course, Kakadu National Park.

WHERE TO START?

At the lower end of **Mitchell Street** you'll find yourself in the thick of things. Highway 1 leads into the city. Parking in the centre is no problem. If you're travelling by train, the station is 15km from the city centre (Berrimah Road) and you have to take a shuttle bus or taxi. The same applies for travellers who arrive at the airport, which is 12km away.

SIGHTSEEING

WATERFRONT

The newly designed harbour is the cherry on the cake that is modern Darwin. There are two palm-fringed lagoons where you can cool down – *Recreation Lagoon*, free entry, is surrounded by cafés, restaurants and boutiques. Try, for instance, *The Precinct (daily from 10am | tel. 08 89 41 90 00 | precincttavern.com.au | $-$$)*, where you can enjoy cold beer and good food on the veranda.

AQUASCENE FISH FEEDING

Every day at high tide, fish come to the shoreline at Doctor's Gully to be fed. It's an excellent opportunity to see catfish, mullet and rays up close. *heck high tide times | $17, children A$12 | 28 Doctors Gully Rd | aquascene.com.au | 1–2 hrs*

BOTANIC GARDENS

In 1870, the gardener Maurice Holtz laid out Darwin's magnificent botanic park. The gardens contain more than 400 species of palm tree that partly grow in a miniature rainforest, a small orchid nursery and an artificial waterfall and swamps. Covering 42,000m², it is one of the botanic gardens with the greatest variety of species in the Southern Hemisphere. *Daily 7am–7pm | admission free | Gilruth Av/ Gardens Rd | short.travel/aus16*

MUSEUM & ART GALLERY OF THE NORTHERN TERRITORY

Rock art dating back more than 40,000 years – how many art museums can

Relax on Darwin's waterfront, complete with bathing lagoon

compete with that? You'll also find contemporary Aboriginal art.

And then there's a cyclone named Tracy. Back in 1974, Cyclone Tracy swept through Darwin at Christmas, razing the city virtually to the ground.

INSIDER TIP **Cyclone experience**

Experience the huge acoustic force of the hurricane in the darkroom. Exhibits from the 50th anniversary exhibition showcase a dark sense of humour.

The *Darwin Ski Club (daily | darwinskiclub.com.au | $$)*, opposite, has an excellent beer garden. *Daily 10am–4pm | admission free | Conacher St, Fannie Bay | magnt.net.au | 1–2 hrs*

EATING & DRINKING

As well as in the harbour quarter, you will find lots of restaurants on *Mitchell Street* and at *Cullen Bay Marina*.

HANUMAN

Asian cuisine dominates Darwin's culinary landscape. One of the top stops is Hanuman, which serves a fusion of predominantly Indian and Thai flavours. *Dinner daily from 6pm, lunch Wed–Fri only | 93 Mitchell St | tel. 08 89 41 35 00 | $$*

PEE WEE'S

Here, under palm trees and with a great view of Fannie Bay, you can indulge in creative Australian food and good wines. *Tue–Sat from 4pm | Alec Fong Lim Drive, East Point | tel. 08 89 81 68 68 | peewees.com.au | $$$*

SHOPPING

Darwin is well known for its many markets, e.g. the *Parap Village Markets (Sat 8am–2pm | Parap Rd)*, the *Mindil Beach Sunset Market (see p. 114)* and the *Rapid Creek Market (Sat/Sun 7am–2pm | Rapid Creek Business Village | 48 Trower Rd | approx. 20 mins from the city).* The Territory's cultured pearls are available from *Paspaley Pearls (Bennett Street/Smith Street Mall).* The best address for freshly caught fish is *Frances Bay:* At *Mr Barra (shop 20 | mrbarra.com.au)* behind Fisherman's Wharf and in *Darwin Fish Market (shop 5 | access via Frances Bay Drive | darwinfishmarket.com),* the seafood and shellfish displays will make your mouth water.

Mason Gallery (7/21 Cavenagh St | masongallery.com.au) is one of Darwin's best art galleries. *Aboriginal Fine Arts (11 Knuckey St | aaia.com.au)* sells certified Aboriginal art. Note: if shipping to Europe, works of art are subject to tax based on their value!

SPORT & ACTIVITIES

EAST POINT RESERVE

The park on the beach close to the city centre is a popular place for picnics and relaxing and for swimming in Lake Alexander, a saltwater basin that is free of stinger jellyfish all year round. During the rainy season, the lake is sometimes closed if the bacteria levels get too high.

CROCODILE CRUISE

While you might be interested in seeing some of the Northern Territory's most fascinating inhabitants, a surprise meeting is probably not the best way! Put your mind at rest with a one-hour tour on the Adelaide River. Tours run several times a day and provide a chance to get up close and personal with the reptiles. *A$50, children A$35, families from A$145 | jumpingcrocodile.com.au*

BEACHES

MINDIL BEACH

The quickest way to make friends back home envious: send them a picture of the tropical sun sinking into the sea on Mindil Beach, a 20-minute walk from the city, or on market days, take bus no.4 or no.6. On Thursdays, the legendary sunset is celebrated at the *Mindil Beach Sunset Market (April–Oct 5–10pm | mindil.com.au)* with reasonably priced food stands, fine arts and crafts, street performers and the sounds of the didgeridoo.

WATCH OUT – CROC ABOUT!

Salties is the almost affectionate nickname for saltwater crocodiles, which not only live in large numbers along the coasts in the far north of Australia, but also feel completely at home in the *billabongs* (waterholes) of the national parks. As you are certain to come off worse in an encounter with one of these sharp-toothed saurians, please do not ignore this absolute rule:

"Only bathe where it is explicitly permitted."

Barramundi versus saltwater crocodile

NIGHTLIFE

DECKCHAIR CINEMA

Darwin really comes to life once the sun sets. The open-air cinema runs from April to November and has 250 deckchairs and 100 seats. Food and drinks are available (incl. beer and wine) but be sure to take good insect protection with you. *Performance times, see website | Jervois Rd, Waterfront | deckchaircinema.com.au*

SUNSET CRUISE

With such wonderful sunsets, an atmospheric boat trip in the late afternoon around the extensive harbour bay is a good idea. Perhaps combine it with a delicious dinner on board the nostalgic schooner *Alfred Nobel*. This will be accompanied by good wine, a refreshing breeze and wonderful views of the tropical coastline. *Darwin Harbour Cruises (daily at sunset | A$125 | from Stokes Wharf | tel. 08 89 42 31 31 | darwinharbourcruises.com.au).*

AROUND DARWIN

1 TERRITORY WILDLIFE PARK

50km / 40 mins from Darwin by car

This large park provides a very good insight into the fauna and flora of the Northern Territory and allows you to get up close and personal with the park's animal inhabitants. Demonstrations (with birds of prey, for example) take place multiple times a day. *Daily 9am–5pm | A$40, children A$20 | Berry Springs | territory wildlifepark.com.au | 3 hrs | D1*

2 LITCHFIELD NATIONAL PARK ★

122km / 1½ hrs from Darwin by car

This national park is a wild oasis with waterfalls, gorges, rainforest and huge termite mounds. You can swim in a number of waterholes without having to worry about crocodiles. The *Wangi*

Falls and *Florence Falls* are particularly beautiful – and are great for swimming. There are several simple campsites in the vicinity.

If there's a creature that knows a thing or two about building, it's the compass termite; check out the *Magnetic Termite Mounds*, just outside the small town of Bachelor. The impressive structures look like tombstones against the landscape. *Admission free | short.travel/aus50 |* 🕮 *D1*

3 TIWI ISLANDS

80km / 2½ hrs from Darwin by ferry

Off the coast of Darwin are *Melville* and *Bathurst*, two islands whose inhabitants have retained their own distinct culture and are well known for their craftwork and painting. Tourism is carefully regulated. The once-a-day boat trip goes to Bathurst, the main island, where you'll be able to meet the local residents. Bookings through *Sealink (day tour from A$470 | sealinknt.com.au).* 🕮 *D–E1*

KAKADU NATIONAL PARK

(🕮 *E1)* ★ **Kakadu National Park is an important site for local Aboriginal people, who have called this unique, rugged land home for tens of thousands of years.**

Fiery red rocks, waterfalls, billabongs teeming with lurking crocodiles, ancient rock paintings, and a generous dose of mysticism await you in this protected area, which is possibly Australia's most famous national park,

The almost 20,000km² UNESCO World Heritage Site can be reached along the surfaced Arnhem Highway in a conventional car outside of the wet season. The main centre of the park is *Jabiru*, where you can find accommodation that will suit all budgets. The best time to go is during the dry season (May–October) and allow at least two to three days. *Pass A$40/ pers valid for 7 days, available from the Visitor Centre or online: kakadu.gov.au.*

Experiences include a foray through the park with ⚑ *Animal Tracks Safari (day trip A$220 | animaltracks.com.au)*, and the *Guluyambi Cultural Cruise (2 hrs | A$89 | kakaduculturaltours.com.au)*, a boat trip along the East Alligator River into Arnhem Land. You will be accompanied by an Aboriginal guide on both trips.

SIGHTSEEING

BOWALI VISITOR CENTRE

The tourist information centre just outside Jabiru is the first port of call for the national park. It contains a good exhibition on the history of the region, in parts related by local people, as well as maps and other aids to orientation. It also issues the obligatory park pass. ⏲ *1 hr*

ROCK PAINTINGS

He's been lying there like that, naked and with his legs apart, for thousands of years. "X-ray man" is one of the best-known rock paintings; some 250,000 visitors admire him every year on the short walk to *Nourlangie Rock (daily from 8am until sunset)*. It's much quieter at the no less impressive rock paintings of *Ubirr* on the East Alligator River. A circular walk leads up to a 250m-high plateau that offers wonderful views of the alluvial land.

INSIDER TIP
Rock art without the crowds

YELLOW WATER BILLABONG

A boat trip across the Yellow River at sunrise or sunset against the backdrop of the twittering of countless birds, is like a massage for the soul … until the idyll is rudely interrupted by a snapping crocodile that suddenly appears beside the boat! *Bookable from Cooinda Lodge | from A$105 | tel. 08 89 79 15 00 | kakadutourism.com.*

Be sure to visit the nearby *Warradjan Aboriginal Cultural Centre (daily 9am–5pm | admission free)* dedicated to local Indigenous culture.

JIM JIM FALLS & TWIN FALLS

We recommend an all-terrain vehicle for this 70km detour from Kakadu Highway – and it's only possible during the dry season. The attractions include the *Jim Jim Falls*, which are over 200m high, and even deeper in the bush are the equally impressive *Twin Falls*. Having said that, from about June the Jim Jim waterfalls dwindle to little more than a trickle *(day tours A$355 | kakadutoursandtravel.com.au/tour/jim-jim-falls-tour)*. One alternative during the rainy season is an hour-long sightseeing flight from Jabiru with *Kakadu Air (A$355 | kakaduair.com.au)*.

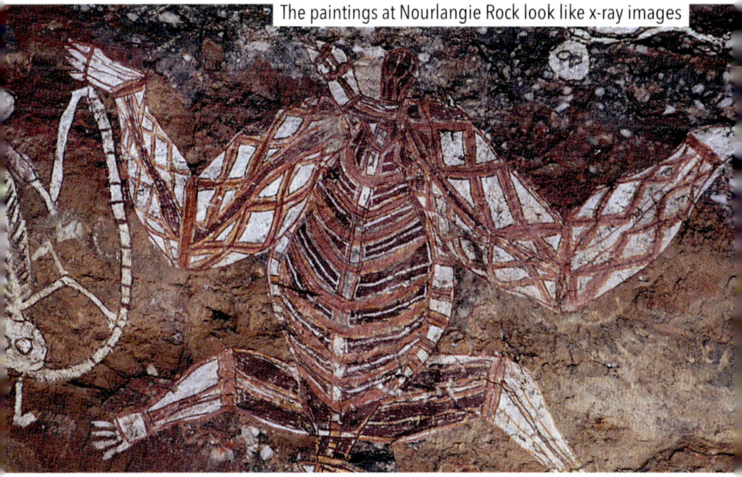
The paintings at Nourlangie Rock look like x-ray images

Spectacular Nitmiluk (Katherine Gorge)

KATHERINE

(🕮 E1–2) **Whichever direction you are arriving from, the little town of Katherine (pop. 6,500) will initially feel like a metropolitan city.**

So, brush off the dust of the outback, refuel the car, and then admire the tremendous array of food in the supermarket. And if, after a few days, you feel drawn back to the landscape of the Northern Territory, drive through the Nitmiluk National Park with the Edith Falls and spectacular Katherine Gorge.

AROUND KATHERINE

5 NITMILUK NATIONAL PARK

28km / ½ hr from Katherine by car

For millions of years, the Katherine River has burrowed its way through the sandstone plateau, forming a system of 13 gorges in total. At 28km long ★ *Nitmiluk (Katherine Gorge)* reveals its magic quite spectacularly when the sun hangs low in the sky. Hire a canoe *(Nitmiluk Tours | single canoe A$120, double canoe A$220, incl. shuttle to third gorge | tel. 013 00 14 67 43 | nitmiluktours.com.au)* or walk the *Baruwei Loop Walk* to the lookout platform (approx. 1½ hours). Real outdoor enthusiasts can hire a canoe for two days *(single canoe A$220, double canoe A$400)* to give themselves enough time to paddle to

AROUND KAKADU NATIONAL PARK

4 ARNHEM LAND

Trips to Arnhem Land, a largely under-explored area and one of the final frontiers for mass tourism, are well worthwhile. The Yolngu and other First Peoples have native title rights to much of Arnhem Land. For cultural reasons, access is granted to only a small number of visitors. Tours and information: *Arnhemlander Cultural & Heritage Tour (kakaduculturaltours.com.au).* *🕮 E2* the sixth or seventh gorge, where there are campsites.

The *Edith Falls* are also well worth the detour from Stuart Highway. They cascade into a pool surrounded by palm trees, where swimming is delightful. Occasionally, you can join a tour with a ranger, and there is also a lovely campsite and a small kiosk. *E1*

INSIDER TIP
Swim under palm trees

ALICE SPRINGS

(E4) **It isn't possible for anyone to choose a more remote spot for a town: "The Alice" – as the approx. 25,000 residents call it – is about 1,500km from both Darwin and Adelaide, and almost 3,000km from Sydney.**

The town was established in 1872 as a telegraph station to connect Port Augusta and Darwin. Today, the station is a fascinating open-air museum, yet most of the 500,000-plus tourists who come to Alice Springs every year are drawn straight on to the breathtaking landscape of the Red Centre.

SIGHTSEEING

ANZAC HILL

From here you have a good view over the city. The MacDonnell Ranges in the background turn a wonderful red at sunrise and sunset.

ROYAL FLYING DOCTOR SERVICE

A birth in the bush? An emergency in an outback community? How can medical assistance be given if you're 1,000km from the nearest hospital? Find out here. Incidentally, your admission charge is an important source of income for the Flying Doctor Service. *Daily 9am–4pm | A$20 | 8–10 Stuart Terrace | rfdalicesprings.com.au | 1 ½ hrs*

SCHOOL OF THE AIR

There's a lot of space in the world's largest classroom: 1.3 million km². Children in the outback get their lessons from hundreds of miles away now in their own homes via the internet (formerly via radio). Here you'll gain insights into a childhood deep in the wilderness of the red continent. *Mon–Sat 8.30am–4.30pm, Sun from 1.30pm | A$14.50 | 80 Head St | schooloftheair.net.au | 1 hr*

TELEGRAPH STATION

This lovingly renovated telegraph station, built of hewn rock in 1872, takes you back to Australia's pioneering days. The entry fee includes a guided tour. *Daily 9am–5pm | A$16 | North Stuart Highway | alicespringstelegraphstation.com.au | 1–1 ½ hrs*

ALICE SPRINGS DESERT PARK

If you have always wanted to trek through Australia's fascinating desert landscape, then this one's for you. The huge area gives a good idea of the natural history of the surrounding desert. One highlight is the Nocturnal House – home to a whole range of endangered desert dwellers. Night is definitely the liveliest time here, and you can experience it first hand on the *Nocturnal Tour (A$30)*. *Daily 7.30am–6pm | A$40, children A$20 | Larapinta Drive | alicespringsdesertpark.com.au | 2–3 hrs*

INSIDER TIP
Night at the animal park

KANGAROO SANCTUARY

When travelling through Australia's Red Centre, it is highly likely that you'll see dead kangaroos at the side of the road that have been hit by vehicles. Often a dead female might have a joey in her pouch that has survived the accident but needs ongoing care. At the Kangaroo Sanctuary, 15km from Alice Springs, the young are given medical attention and, wherever possible, released back into the wild. *Feb–Nov daily tours from Alice Springs | A$105, children A$95 | kangaroosanctuary.com | 3 hrs*

SHOPPING

An Aboriginal dot painting created in the surrounding desert communities, such as Utopia and of Papunya, is not only a beautiful souvenir, but - depending on the artist - can also be an investment. They are sold, for example, at the *Mbantua Gallery (24 Elder St | mbantua.com.au)*. For more expensive pieces, be sure to request a certificate of authenticity! For more information, see *desart.com.au*.

NIGHTLIFE

The Rock Bar (78 Todd St) is a good place for a drink, as is *Todd Tavern (1 Todd Mall)*. But a word of warning: there have been repeated confrontations between drunken locals and tourists, especially at night.

AROUND ALICE SPRINGS

6 HERMANNSBURG

127km / 1½ hrs from Alice Springs by car

This village west of Alice Springs (pop. 550) has a former Lutheran *missionary station (daily 9am–5pm | A$19 | 1 hr)* that was founded in 1877. The informative and moving exhibition is a reminder of controversial attempts by the church to convert Indigenous Australians to Christianity by trying to enforce values of "order and discipline".

Well-known former residents of Hermannsburg include the painter Albert Namatjira (1902–59), founder of a rather Western landscape painting style of the outback (the Hermannsburg School), and ethnologist Ted Strehlow (1908–78), leading researcher of the culture of the Central Australian Arrarnta people. *hermannsburg.com.au* | *E4*

7 KINGS CANYON (WATARRKA) ★

470km / 6 hrs from Alice Springs by car

The steep gorge with its weathered peaks today attracts almost as many visitors as Uluru. But do not miss Kings Canyon. There are asphalted roads from Alice Springs or Erldunda, and from Uluru via the *Lasseter Highway* and *Luritja Road*, to this rocky landscape, which is millions of years old. Alternatively, take the route along *Larapinta Drive* via Hermannsburg, which should only be tackled in a 4WD. You need to be fairly fit for the three-to four-hour ✓ *Canyon Walk* around the gorge. It's best to start early in the morning – and be sure to take plenty of water with you! If that sounds a bit too much like hard work, the 45-minute *Kings Creek Walk* is easier and has more shade. *E4*

Art for sale in Alice Springs

8 ULURU-KATA TJUTA NATIONAL PARK ★

468km / 5¾ hrs from Alice Springs by car

The 348m-high monolith known as Uluru, rather like an iceberg, reaches miles down into the ground beneath. It attracts hundreds of thousands of visitors every year to the red heart of the continent. For Anangu people, however, it is the site with the greatest spiritual meaning and an important testimony to their creation story. In 1985, land encompassing Uluru and "neighbouring" Kata Tjuta was made into a national park covering 1,325km² and returned to the Anangu.

The entrance to the park *(A$38/ pers)* is about 15km from Uluru. There are two viewing areas along this stretch from where you can watch the sunrise or sunset. Please note: alcohol is forbidden (although organised tour groups are exempted). There are also several car parks at Uluru itself from which you can explore the base of the rock. Overnight stays are not permitted in the national park. The *Ayers Rock Resort (ayersrockresort.com.au)* in *Yulara* is the supply centre for Uluru, approx. 15km from the rock and 6km from the airport. It has restaurants, a supermarket, booking offices, souvenir and textile shops, hotels of every category, and a campsite. There are shuttle buses between Alice Springs and Ayers Rock Resort *(approx. 5½ hrs | A$250 one way | emurun.com.au)*.

Climbing Uluru, which is sacred to the Anangu, is strictly forbidden. In any case, it's more beautiful from below: the 10km Base Walk takes you round the monolith in about three hours. Park rangers offer free guided walks *(daily Oct–April 8am, May–Sept 10am | from Mala Walk Car Park)*. You'll find many other tours and activities, some free of charge, at the *Tours & Information Centre (daily 8am–7pm)* of the Ayers Rock Resort (Yulara). On the *SEIT Uluru Tour (5 hrs | A$220)*, for instance, the mythology associated with the rock is explained, and visitors are shown how local Anangu people have survived in this apparently inhospitable land for millennia.

At the *Uluru-Kata Tjuta Cultural Centre (daily 7am–6pm | admission free | short.travel/aus15)*, you can find out what other activities are available in the national park, visit an interesting exhibition on Anangu culture and see the nature in the park. It is the perfect starting point for a visit to Uluru.

The *Wintjiri Wiru Sunset Dinner (A$310 | short.travel/aus63)* sees light artists transform Uluru into a performance stage while you enjoy cocktails and dishes made with local bush ingredients. As darkness falls, luminous lasers, projections and drones tell Anangu stories in a breathtaking choreography, accompanied by Indigenous music. Not far away, a carpet of 50,000 lights, installed by British-Australian artist Bruce Munro, illuminates the site every evening *(Field of Light | from A$48 | short.travel/aus64)*.

INSIDER TIP
Dining with drones

About 50km from Uluru is *Kata Tjuta*, a collection of 36 rounded, domed rocks over an area of 35km². The highest of these "heads" (*Kata Tjuta* means "many heads") is almost 200m higher than Uluru, and just as impressive. Enjoy the rich orange hues of the Central Australian desert on a lovely walk through the mountains. A hike through the *Valley of the Winds* takes around three hours and is particularly recommended. But don't underestimate the weather: in the cooler months, icy winds howl through the gorges (be sure to take a coat and hat); in summer, the high temperatures turn the rocks into a gigantic oven, so it's best to set off early in the

You can't climb it, but a walk around the base of Uluru is well worth it

morning with plenty of water and an insect net for your head! A shorter walk (about an hour) that is still breathtaking, especially in spring when wildflowers carpet the ground, is the *Walpa Gorge Walk* E4

SLEEP WELL IN THE NORTHERN TERRITORY

SNOOZE BY THE CANYON

A glass of wine in hand, a soft mattress to lie on and the rugged bushland all around. Granted, it's more glamping than camping here, 36km from Kings Canyon. *Kings Creek Station (tel. 08 89 56 74 74 | kingscreek station.com.au | $-$$)* offers three luxury tents and 25 cabins, as well as a more traditional tent area.

POOL PLUS BAR AT KAKADU

The point that some maps call Cooinda actually only refers to *Cooinda Lodge (tel. 08 89 79 15 00 | kakadutourism.com | $-$$$)*. You have the choice of 48 rooms and a lovely campsite, and everything is arranged around a central pool with a bar and restaurant.

WESTERN AUSTRALIA

THE VASTNESS IS UTTERLY AWE-INSPIRING

Were you to divide the land area of Western Australia – WA for short – equally among its population, then every single individual, from the tiniest baby to the oldest senior citizen, would have their very own square kilometre.

Slightly less than 2.6 million people live on the 2.5 million km² of this land mass, which is one-third of the entire continent. The region is as varied as it is vast, ranging from the fabulous surfing beaches

Nambung National Park is an other-worldly landscape in the desert

and idyllic wine-growing areas in the south, to bizarre landscapes such as the Pinnacles, Karijini National Park and Purnululu National Park, and isolated Ningaloo Reef and the Kimberleys, in the north.

From cosmopolitan Perth, you can comfortably explore the south-west in a week or two. A trip to the vast, almost uninhabited north promises fabulous highlights, but allow at least four weeks for the route from Perth to Darwin.

WESTERN AUSTRALIA

MARCO POLO BUCKET LIST

7 ✓ Meet friendly giants

The world's largest fish are gentle giants. Snorkel with whale sharks on the *Ningaloo Reef* ➤ p. 135

8 ✓ Drive a 4WD through the wilderness

One thousand kilometres of adventure on the *Gibb River Road* through the Kimberley region ➤ p. 140

If possible, plan your trip so that you're in Broome for a full moon. The phenomenon known as the "Staircase to the Moon" can be seen here between March and October.

Your best chance of coming face to face with a whale shark is between March and July in the sea around Exmouth.

If you have enough time, consider walking from Cape Naturaliste to Cape Leeuwin on the Cape to Cape Track: 135km along the coast over eight days.

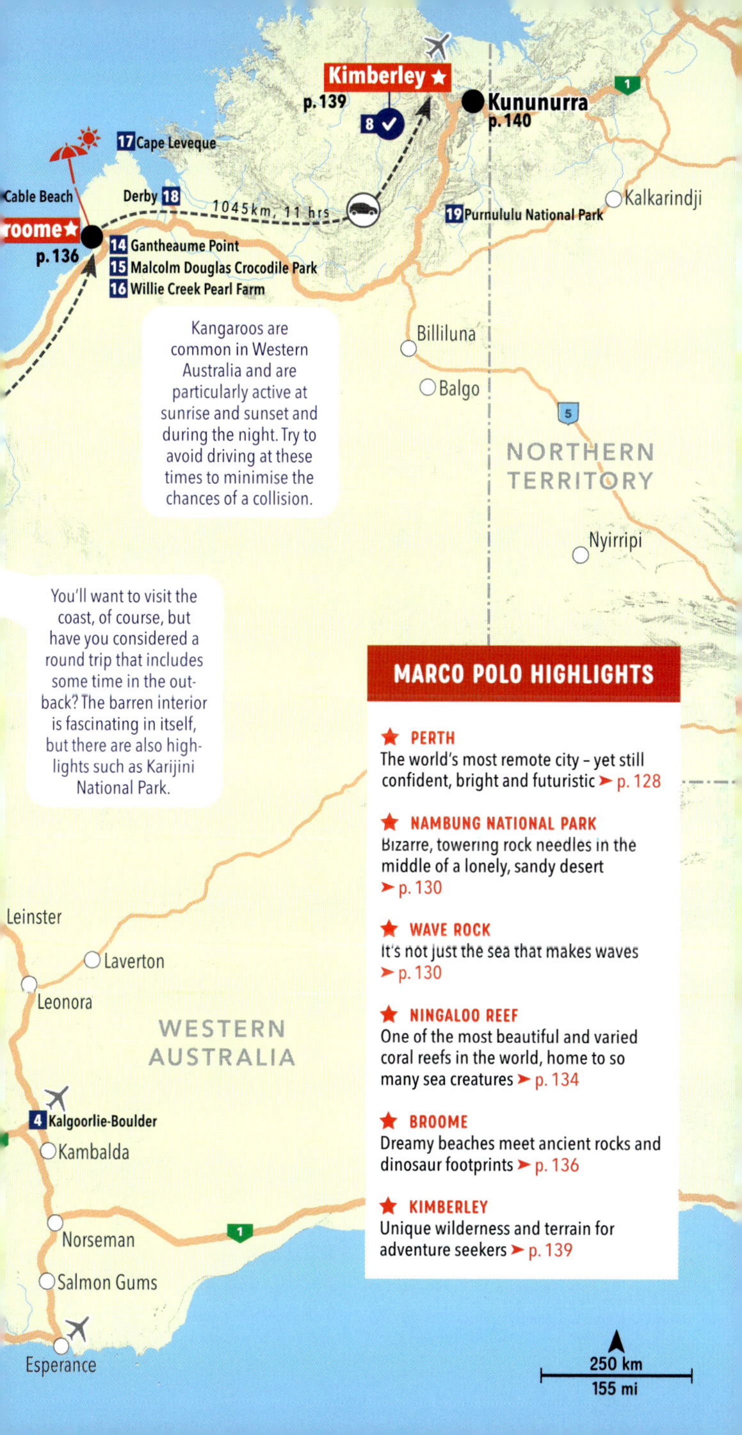

Kangaroos are common in Western Australia and are particularly active at sunrise and sunset and during the night. Try to avoid driving at these times to minimise the chances of a collision.

You'll want to visit the coast, of course, but have you considered a round trip that includes some time in the outback? The barren interior is fascinating in itself, but there are also highlights such as Karijini National Park.

MARCO POLO HIGHLIGHTS

★ **PERTH**
The world's most remote city – yet still confident, bright and futuristic ➤ p. 128

★ **NAMBUNG NATIONAL PARK**
Bizarre, towering rock needles in the middle of a lonely, sandy desert ➤ p. 130

★ **WAVE ROCK**
It's not just the sea that makes waves ➤ p. 130

★ **NINGALOO REEF**
One of the most beautiful and varied coral reefs in the world, home to so many sea creatures ➤ p. 134

★ **BROOME**
Dreamy beaches meet ancient rocks and dinosaur footprints ➤ p. 136

★ **KIMBERLEY**
Unique wilderness and terrain for adventure seekers ➤ p. 139

PERTH

(ꝏ B6) **Thanks to its modern skyline and a futuristic beach promenade, your first impression of ★ Perth (pop. 2.3 million) may well be that of a Gulf metropolis.**

Since the beginning of the 21st century, a boom in raw materials has seen Perth grow rapidly, but Western Australia's capital remains what it has always been: an attractive and relaxed city that is a great place to live, with lots of sunshine and nature-loving locals who are only too happy to exchange shirt and tie for a Neoprene wetsuit and surfboard. You can get to *Cottesloe Beach*, one of the loveliest city beaches, from the city centre in about 30 minutes by train and bus.

Four free bus routes serve Perth's centre *(Free Transit Zone | short.travel/aus21)*: the red and yellow CAT buses run east to west; the blue run north to south and the green are in the west.

WHERE TO START?

Many sights can be reached on foot from the pedestrianised **City Mall** *(Murray Street/Hay Street)*, including Yagan Square, the new Elizabeth Quay and the City Railway Station, where regional trains also stop, e.g. from Fremantle. The bus terminal is opposite the station. You can leave your car at your accommodation, as there are free buses in the city.

SIGHTSEEING

KINGS PARK

Get a first impression of Perth from the park's many lookouts and climb the *DNA Observation Tower*. The lovely botanical garden behind the park is an oasis of peace with a café and gift shop. Indigenous guides offer tours *(bgpa.wa.gov.au/culturaltours)*. *bgpa.wa.gov.au/kings-park*

ELIZABETH QUAY

The former harbour is today a futuristic waterfront space complete with art island, water parks, bars and restaurants. Elizabeth Quay is evidence of Western Australia's abundant natural resources and their unabashed exploitation. The *Bell Tower (Tue–Sun 10am–2pm | A$15 | Barrack Sq | thebelltower.com.au)* on neighbouring Barrack Square is also worth a visit.

PERTH MINT

This is where you can see the world's largest collection of gold nuggets and watch while the precious metal is cast. *Daily 9am–5pm | A$25 | 310 Hay St | perthmint.com.au. | 1½ hrs*

FREMANTLE

The best time to visit this pretty harbour city is at the weekend, when the stalls of *Fremantle Market (Fri–Sun 8am–6pm | Henderson St/South Terrace | freemantlemarkets.com.au)* fill the air with the aromas of coffee and curry, street performers keep you smiling, and everything from juicy fruit to stylish clothing is on sale. You can reach Fremantle either by train or

boat from Barrack Street Jetty in Perth. The main attraction is *Fremantle Prison (daily 9am–5pm | tour A$23 | The Terrace | fremantleprison.com.au | ⏲ 1–2 hrs)*, where, for over 140 years, Western Australia's most dangerous criminals languished. *visitfremantle.com.au*

EATING & DRINKING

BATHERS BEACH HOUSE

Seafood on your plate, a cocktail in your hand and sand between your toes. You're advised to book the beach sun-loungers in advance. *Daily from 11am | 44B Mews Rd, Fremantle | tel. 08 93 35 29 11 | bathersbeachhouse.com.au | $$*

COTTESLOE BEACH HOTEL

Choose between fine dining or fish and chips with a beer on the terrace. Either way you'll have a view over the beach. There are local craft beers on tap in the bar. *Daily from 11am | 104 Marine Parade, Cottesloe | tel. 08 93 83 11 00 | cottesloebeachhotel.com.au | $–$$*

FRASER'S RESTAURANT

It's hard to say which is better: the view or the food. The top address for special occasions (you're sure to think of one) offers fabulous views of Kings Park and the city. Try the melt-in-the-mouth fresh squid. *Daily | Fraser Av, Kings Park | tel. 08 94 81 71 00 | frasersrestaurant.com.au | $$$*

INSIDER TIP
For seafood fans

SHOPPING

The *Forrest Chase (200 Murray St | forrestchase.com.au)* shopping complex offers endless opportunities to update your wardrobe.

NIGHTLIFE

For concerts and events, scroll through the gig guide in Perth's online magazine *Xpress (xpressmag.com.au/ events)*. Nightlife is largely concentrated in the *Subiaco* district *(Hay St)*.

METRO CITY

Live music and clubbing: there's always something going on at this giant venue. *For details, see the website | 146 Roe St, Northbridge | metroconcertclub.com*

AROUND PERTH

1 ROTTNEST ISLAND

18km / 1½ hrs from Perth by ferry

The only habitat of the quokka, a marsupial that looks like it's always smiling thanks to its narrow jaw and overbite. The best way to visit these relatives of the kangaroo is by ferry *(return ticket A$100 | rottnestexpress.com.au)*. Cars aren't allowed on the island, but you can easily reach the beautiful beaches by bike, which can be hired from the visitor centre. *Rottnest Island Visitor Centre | tel. 08 94 32 93 00 | rottnest island.com |* *B6*

2 NAMBUNG NATIONAL PARK ★

190km / 2 hrs 20 mins from Perth by car

A paradise for photographers, both amateur and professional. This spectacular collection of limestone pillars in the Nambung National Park is best visited early in the morning for perfect light conditions. Some of the Pinnacles look like people turned to stone, which you can best appreciate if you take the 5km circuit route through the forest of pillars or pose for a photo between the boulders – the story can seem really believable..

INSIDER TIP **Pillars at sunrise**

It has been worked out that the Pinnacles – some up to 5m high – were created between 80,000 to 150,000 years ago during a particularly wet period for the region. The abundance of water caused the limestone to dissolve, resulting in the iron-rich pillars you see today. *A5*

3 WAVE ROCK ★

340km / 3¾ hrs from Perth by car

Who says waves can only exist in water? Wave Rock is an imposing rock formation shaped like a 15m-high wave, 340km southeast of Perth near the town of Hyden. This huge wave was created by the wind and weather: heat, frost and flood waters that, over the course of time, left their mark in the form of strange striped patterns. Wave Rock is more than two million years old. *B6*

4 KALGOORLIE-BOULDER

600km / 6½ hrs from Perth by car

Granted, a trip from Perth to the goldfields in the east is more than a mere excursion. But if you happen to be on your way to South Australia or the Red Centre, why not stop to see the precious metal for yourself? Discovered in 1892, the gold reserves are still one of the main reasons for the affluence of Western Australia today. The area is characterised by open-cut mines, which are best explored on a guided tour. *Kalgoorlie-Boulder Tourist Centre | tel. 08 90 21 19 66 | kalgoorlietourism.com)* | *C5*

MARGARET RIVER

(B6) **Waves, wine and wellness: in only 50 years, the idyllic provincial town of Margaret River (pop. 10,200), close to the breathtaking coast, has become a first-class wine-growing region.**

Many of the area's 200 wineries offer wine tasting and some also have excellent restaurants. Paths lead through secluded woods; you can find beaches with sensational surfing along the rocky coast between Cape Naturaliste and Cape Leeuwin, with more sheltered bathing spots around sandy Geographe Bay. Between June and December whales visit the coastal

The sculptural power of nature is on display at Wave Rock

Find your favourite tipple at one of the many wineries and breweries around Margaret River

waters and, with a bit of luck, you can sometimes see them from the shore.

EATING & DRINKING

CBCO BREWING

Why not take home one of the various types of home-brewed beer, including *Kolsch Ale*, which is very similar to the German beer of a similar name. It's available in bottles to take away or to be drunk in the pub or in its lovely beer garden – you could even stop for lunch, sometimes with live music on Sundays. *Mon–Thu until 5pm, Fri–Sun until 8pm | Osmington Rd | tel. 08 97 58 81 77 | cbco.beer | $–$$*

MARGARET RIVER CHOCOLATE COMPANY

A must for the sweet-toothed, but also a treat for fans of all things spicy. In this small factory (with a café), the delicious chocolate is sometimes mixed with spices such as chilli pepper. *415 Harman's Mill | chocolatefactory.com.au*

SHOPPING

ART

Many artists and craftspeople have settled in this attractive area. Most studios and galleries are between Margaret River and Yallingup or Dunsborough. A small selection of exquisite, high-quality objects is on sale in *Yallingup Galleries (Caves Road/Gunyulgup Valley Road)*, including works by the contemporary artist Judy Prosser, whose work incorporates Aboriginal motifs. *margaret river.com/things-to-do/arts-culture.au*.

WINE

The *Regional Wine Centre (75 Bussel Highway | mrwines.com)* provides a good overview of the location of local wineries and the wines they produce. A tasting session (and lunch) can be recommended at *Hamelin Bay Wines (199 McDonald Rd | Karridale | approx. 32km to the south)*, with a beautiful view from the dining terrace. Also good is the stylish winery *Leeuwin Estate (Stevens Rd | leeuwinestate.com.au)*, which has an art gallery and an excellent restaurant *(daily 10am–5pm | tel 08 97 59 00 00 | $$)*.

AROUND MARGARET RIVER

5 CAPE LEEUWIN

51km / 40 mins from Margaret River by car

Bussel Highway leads to the infamous rocky headland in the south feared by seafarers and battered by breakers. Beyond Augusta, the last settlement of any size, the tall slim *lighthouse (daily 9am–5pm | A$8, guided tour A$22 | booking tel. 08 97 57 74 11 | short.travel/aus46 | ⏲ 1 hr)* comes into sight. A guided tour will take you up to the all-round lookout with breathtaking distant views. *B6*

6 YALLINGUP

42km / 40 mins from Margaret River by car

Finally: the perfect wave. Yallingup's beaches are the stuff of legend in surfing circles. Don't worry, you don't have to be a pro surfer to make the most of this pretty coastal village. The beaches were practically made for dreamy walks; keep your eyes peeled – dolphins often frolic in the waves here. *B6*

7 CAPE NATURALISTE LIGHTHOUSE

60km / 50 mins from Margaret River by car

The massive lighthouse and the *maritime museum* document the adventurous seafaring history here in Geographe Bay. A guided tour also includes the platform around the lantern room where you gaze far out into the Indian Ocean. Whales can be seen between September and December. *Daily 9am–5pm | A$17 | short.travel/aus47 | ⏲ 1 hr |* *B6*

8 BUSSELTON

40km / 40 mins from Margaret River by car

White sandy beaches have made this coastal town (pop. 43,000) a popular place for a summer break. There are enough good places to stay here at *Geographe Bay* for a few relaxing days. The pier that extends 1.8km into the sea is the longest in the Southern Hemisphere. A small railway along its length takes you to the *Underwater Observatory (daily 9am–5pm | A$40 incl. train ride | busseltonjetty.com.au |*

2 hrs) where you can get up close to the sea life. Thirteen sculptures have been submerged in the sea around the pier; you can explore these with a dive and snorkel pass (A$4). *B6*

9 BUNBURY

100km / 1¼ hrs from Margaret River by car

The old harbour town of Bunbury (pop. 77,000) is now a popular holiday resort, due in no small part to the tame dolphins that regularly visit the bay. At the *Dolphin Discovery Centre (Nov–April, daily 8am–4pm, boat tours all year round | Koombana Drive | tel. 08 97 91 30 88 | dolphindiscovery.com.au | 1½ hrs)*, you can observe these marine mammals from a boat *(A$65)* or up close in the water *(A$220, book ahead!). visitbunbury.com.au | B6*

LIMESTONE CAVES

There are some 330 caves in the karst landscape around Margaret River. The few that are open to the public are on Caves Road *(margaretriverattractions.com/caves)*. Impressive, especially after rain, is *Lake Cave (daily tours 9am–4pm | A$25 | 18km south or Margaret River | 1 hr)*, a throne room of the underworld. The largest accessible cave is *Jewel Cave (daily tours 9.30am–4pm | A$25 | 35km south of Margaret River | short.travel/aus22 | 1 hr)*, and it is the most popular one simply on account of its glittering illuminations that are turned on at the flick of a switch. A more adventurous option is a guied tour through the stalactites and stalagmites in *Ngilgi Cave (daily 9.30am–4pm | from A$25 | 40km north of Yallingup | short.travel/aus23 | 1 hr). B6*

EXMOUTH

(A4) **The small town of Exmouth (pop. 2,800) at the tip of North West Cape has evolved into a starting point for tourists who want to explore one of the last virtually untouched coral reefs in the world.**

The Ningaloo Reef is a prize jewel in Australia's natural treasure trove. The national park itself is largely untouched, but you'll still find all the usual home comforts in Exmouth, especially at the modern *marina* which has posh hotels and good restaurants.

AROUND EXMOUTH

10 NINGALOO REEF ★

150km / 1 hr 40 mins from Exmouth by car

Ningaloo Reef is widely regarded as one of the best places in the world to dive or snorkel. The 260km-long reef, a UNESCO World Heritage Site since 2011, stretches from the small coastal village of *Coral Bay (coralbay.org)* along the peninsula to the north. Its beauty and variety are absolutely on a par with the Barrier Reef to the east of

Snorkel with giant but harmless whale sharks on Ningaloo Reef

Australia. Ningaloo Reef is home to at least 250 types of coral and 500 species of fish. The confluence of ocean currents rich in nutrients and its proximity to the Continental Shelf explain why there are so many different species. Four species of ocean turtle live on the reef, as do manta rays, humpback whales, dugongs and various kinds of shark. Ningaloo Reef has gained a reputation as being one of the very few places where whale sharks can be watched from close quarters. You can swim with these marine animals that grow to up to 18m long – and "no worries": these huge beasts are plankton eaters and are not dangerous at all.

Ningaloo Reef can be reached on foot from the mainland. In lagoons such as *Turquoise Bay*, 60km south of Exmouth, you can take a look at the variety of coral and fish in waist-deep water equipped with just goggles and a snorkel. Diving tours are organised by tour operators, e.g. *Ningaloo Reef Dive (from A$190 | ningalooreefdive.com)*, to the outer reaches, while ✓ snorkelling expeditions, e.g. with *Whaleshark n Dive (A$350 whalesharktours.com.au)*, visit the whale sharks from April to July. *A4*

11 CAPE RANGE NATIONAL PARK

35km / 45 mins from Exmouth by car

The national park bordering Ningaloo Reef is outstanding due to its number of unique geological features, fossils and its 630 flowering plant species. There are basic but good campsites *(exploreparks.dbca.wa.gov.au)*, or you can take a tour with *Ningaloo Safari Tours (day tour A$250 | 23 Ningaloo St, Exmouth | tel. 08 99 49 15 50 | ningaloosafari.com)* to see the park's beauty. *A4*

12 KARIJINI NATIONAL PARK

640km / 8 hrs from Exmouth by car

Karijini, east of Exmouth, is the second largest national park in the state, covering 6,000km² and, with its orangey-red rock formations, its scenery is considered the most spectacular. Accommodation and dining options are available in *Tom Price* and *Paraburdoo*. Camping is permitted in the park. *short.travel/aus48* | *B4*

13 MONKEY MIA

705km / 7½ hrs from Exmouth by car

In Monkey Mia, halfway between Perth and Exmouth, you can watch dolphins at close quarters. Most mornings the animals swim right next to the beach of the *Monkey Mia Reserve (A$15, families A$35 | sharkbay.org)* and are fed by rangers standing knee-deep in the water. This attracts tens of thousands of visitors to this area of Shark Bay every year, although the feeding of dolphins is a matter of some dispute – critics believe that feeding makes the animals dependent on humans – and it has come under significantly greater restrictions in recent years.

INSIDER TIP **The cradle of life**

At the *Hamelin Pool Marine Nature Reserve (short.travel/aus51)* you will have a unique chance to meet the oldest lifeform on our planet: marine stromatolites. These "living fossils", created by microorganisms and scattered here in the warm ocean, are already a whopping 3.5 billion years old. *A4*

BROOME

(C2) **Sailing yachts glide across the velvety water, and there's camel trekking on the beach. And when the glowing red tropical sun sinks beyond the horizon in Kimberley's secret capital of ★ Broome (pop. 15,000), the town briefly holds it breath.**

This natural spectacle, which happens every evening and attracts both residents and tourists who wait for it with folding chairs and cans of beer, is just one of the reasons why Broome is becoming more and more popular as a travel destination – it is also becoming the chosen home for Australians wishing to escape the winter. In its favour are the pleasant climate and the relaxed, tropical lifestyle of the "pearling town". Until 1920, Broome was the world's leading centre for pearl farming and the production of mother-of-pearl. And although tourism has largely replaced pearl farming as the main industry, those who wish to buy pearls here will still have plenty of choice.

EATING & DRINKING

BAY CLUB

You have to ask yourself what's better: the fabulous views over Roebuck Bay, or the mouth-watering sight of the catch of the day on your plate. The grilled specialities are especially popular. *Daily | 47 Carnavon St (in the Mangrove Resort) | tel. 08 91 92 13 03 | mangrovehotel.com.au | $$–$$$*

A camel ride is a great way to explore the beach in Broome

MATSO'S BREWERY
A legend in Broome. Home-brewed beer, burgers and the best company. *Daily | 60 Hammersly St | tel. 08 91 93 58 11 | matsos.com.au | $$*

SHOPPING

You can purchase pearls from *Willie Creek Pearl Farm* in the centre *(32 Blackman St)* and on Cable Beach *(2 Challenor Drive)*.

BEACHES

CABLE BEACH

This fine sandy beach is 22km long – no wonder it is the town's main attraction. Part of the fun is enjoying a leisurely beach ride on a camel – so make sure to jump into the saddle with *Broome Camel Safaris (from A$35 | broomecamelsafaris.com.au)*, for example. The phenomenon called the *Staircase to the Moon* that can be seen here is a unique natural spectacle. The unforgettable sight occurs between March and October on three days every month, when the full moon is reflected in the grooves left in the sand by the receding tide. Exact dates can be obtained at *short.travel/aus52*.

INSIDER TIP
Staircase to the moon

AROUND BROOME

14 GANTHEAUME POINT

8km / 10 mins from Broome by car

Can rocks really be this red? At the southwestern tip of Broome in front of the turquoise sea, sandstone boulders are stacked in curious piles – a sight well worth the short hike (about 200m from the car park). At extremely low tide, the waves recede to reveal 130-million-year-old dinosaur footprints. Note: the last 2km to the car park are dirt roads and may be impassable during the rainy season. *C2*

15 MALCOLM DOUGLAS CROCODILE PARK

16km / 15 mins from Broome by car

Wildlife film-maker Malcolm Douglas, the real "Crocodile Dundee", made a name for himself catching dangerous saltwater crocodiles. He was killed in a car accident in 2010, but his legacy lives on. In his large park, more than 200 crocodiles and other wild animals can be seen. *Daily 2–5pm, crocodile feeding 3pm | A$40, children A$25, families A$110 | Great Northern Highway | malcolmdouglas.com.au | 2 hrs | C2*

16 WILLIE CREEK PEARL FARM

40km / 50 mins from Broome by car

This pearl farm offers a good introduction into the art of pearl farming. *A$95, 5-hr bus tour from Broome A$149 | tour reservation tel. 08 91 92 00 00 | williecreekpearls.com.au | 1 ½ hrs | C2*

17 CAPE LEVEQUE

208km / 4 hrs from Broome by car

If you're in the mood for an all-terrain adventure, then the Dampier Peninsula is just the place for you. Local Indigenous peoples have been granted native title rights to much of this area. A sand and dust track leads to Cape Leveque, where you can fish or

Leave footsteps in the sand on the isolated beaches around Cape Leveque

sunbathe on deserted beaches. Accommodation options are few and far between, so be sure to book in advance – even the campsite! *C2*

18 DERBY

220km / 2½ hrs from Broome by car

Admittedly, this small town (pop. 3,300) on the edge of the Kimberley region is not all that much to look at and historically it is known for all the wrong reasons too: during World War II, a few Japanese bombs fell in Derby, and in more recent years illegal immigrants have been detained here. But you don't come to Derby for the town, you come for the sensational *Horizontal Waterfalls* in Talbot Bay – a bay dotted with islands, where the strong current sends water shooting through the narrow channels between the sandstone cliffs. There are flights from Broome as well as day tours with, for example, *Horizontal Falls Seaplane Adventures (approx. A$1,100 | horizontalfallsadventures.com.au)*. *C2*

KIMBERLEY

(C-D2) **Only the most adventurous visitors make it to the vast ★ Kimberley region in the north. Massive canyons, waterfalls, endless horizons and unique rock paintings attract people to the far north of Western Australia.**

Huge swathes of this nature reserve, which covers 424,000km² between the towns of Broome in the west and Kununurra in the east, are almost entirely uninhabited. The largely untouched scenery is some of the most beautiful Australia has to offer. A journey through Kimberley is not only time-consuming, but it can also be a real challenge. It's vital you take the time to plan well. For detailed information see the website, *kimberleyaustralia.com*.

Although the Great Northern Highway, which runs 1,000km from Broome to Kununurra, is passable all year round, detours to the countless canyons can only be made in a 4WD vehicle. During the wet season, from November to April, large areas are completely submerged. The best time to travel is May/June and September/October. In July and August many motels and campsites, even in the most remote areas, are fully booked.

The Gibb River Road is only passable in the dry season and in an all-terrain vehicle

SIGHTSEEING

GIBB RIVER ROAD ✓

This unsurfaced road leads to the best-known gorges in the Devonian Reef, the main attractions in the Kimberley region. They are, however, only passable by motor vehicle in the dry season, i.e. not between November and April, and the Gibb River Road should only be tackled in a 4WD. Inform yourself beforehand about its condition at the *Main Road Department (tel. 08 91 68 47 77 | mainroads.wa.gov.au | visit kununurra.com/plan/road-conditions)*.

KUNUNURRA

(🕮 D2) **This small town (pop. 7,500) on the border with the Northern Territory was only built in the 1960s, during the construction of the massive Ord River dam.**

Boat trips are offered on *Lake Argyle*, the reservoir that was created covering more than 1,000km². Venture out to *El Questro Wilderness Park (May–Oct | elquestro.com.au)*, which has a variety of different types of accommodation. Kununurra is the ideal starting point for tours and spectacular scenery is guaranteed.

AROUND KUNUNURRA

19 PURNULULU NATIONAL PARK

291km / 4¼ hrs from Kununurra by car

A visit to this national park is only possible in the dry season, from around May to September. The lichen-streaked, sandstone formations of the *Bungle Bungles* are 300km south of Kununurra and are just as spectacular as Uluru. From the Great Northern Highway, the park can only be reached by all-terrain vehicles, even in good weather, as the dirt track crosses several watercourses. *hallscreektourism.com.au* | *D2*

SLEEP WELL IN WESTERN AUSTRALIA

(NOT) JUST FOR BIRDWATCHERS

The beautiful *BBO Campground (Crab Creek Rd, Roebuck Bay | 6km unsurfaced road | tel. 08 91 93 56 00 | broomebirdobservatory.com | $)* is on Roebuck Bay, approx. 25km from Broome. The campsite might not have electricity, but it does come with some pretty special views: this bird observatory is considered by ornithologists to be one of the five most important in the world.

HIDDEN LUXURY

The *Hidden Valley Forest Retreat (Hagg Rd | approx. 30km north of Margaret River | tel. 08 63 83 98 90 | yourhiddenvalley.com | $$$)*, with four secluded eco-chalets scattered around the bushland, guarantees absolute privacy. And if you don't feel like cooking dinner yourself, the chef will come and conjure up a private gourmet meal.

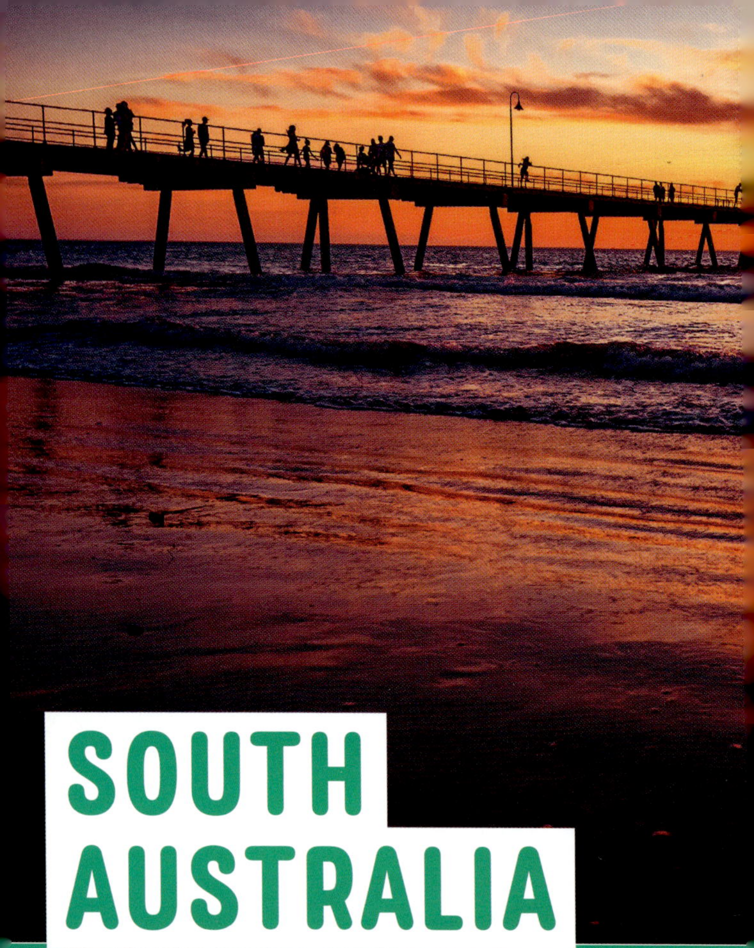

SOUTH AUSTRALIA

DESERT, WINE & BROAD HORIZONS

Kilometres of deserted beaches, exceptional wines, a jam-packed calendar of events, hidden wonders in the desert ... and that's not to mention the wildlife!

Many tourists ignore South Australia, despite there being so many unique treasures and experiences to discover here. Have you ever been cage-diving to see great white sharks, or visited an underground city? And did you know that in the state's mysterious mountains there was once a reef that was home to the world's first living organisms?

Soak up the scenery at Glenelg Beach, just a few minutes from central Adelaide

Around 1.8 million people live in this state, which covers just under one million square kilometres. Most live in the attractive and cultivated capital, Adelaide. But venture beyond the city limits to discover the wildlife of Kangaroo Island, to enjoy the excellent vineyards of the Barossa Valley, to explore the mystical Flinders Ranges, or to encounter dolphins around the unspoilt Eyre Peninsula.

SOUTH AUSTRALIA

MARCO POLO BUCKET LIST

9 ✓ Taste wine that's as old as you are

Sample wines from your birth year on a tour of the *Seppeltsfield Winery* in the Barossa Valley ➤ p. 152

MARCO POLO HIGHLIGHTS

★ **ADELAIDE**
Elegant city of culture between sea and vineyards ➤ p. 146

★ **KANGAROO ISLAND**
An island for animal lovers, with rare species of kangaroo, koalas, sea lions and countless penguins ➤ p. 150

★ **BAROSSA VALLEY**
The legacy of German settlers in wine country ➤ p. 151

★ **EYRE PENINSULA**
Deserted dreamy coastline meets the raw wilderness of the Gawler Ranges ➤ p. 152

★ **IKARA-FLINDERS RANGES NATIONAL PARK**
Red rocks, deep gorges and cave paintings ➤ p. 153

It may not look like much on the map, but Kangaroo Island is more extensive than it first appears. Plan to spend at least two nights here.

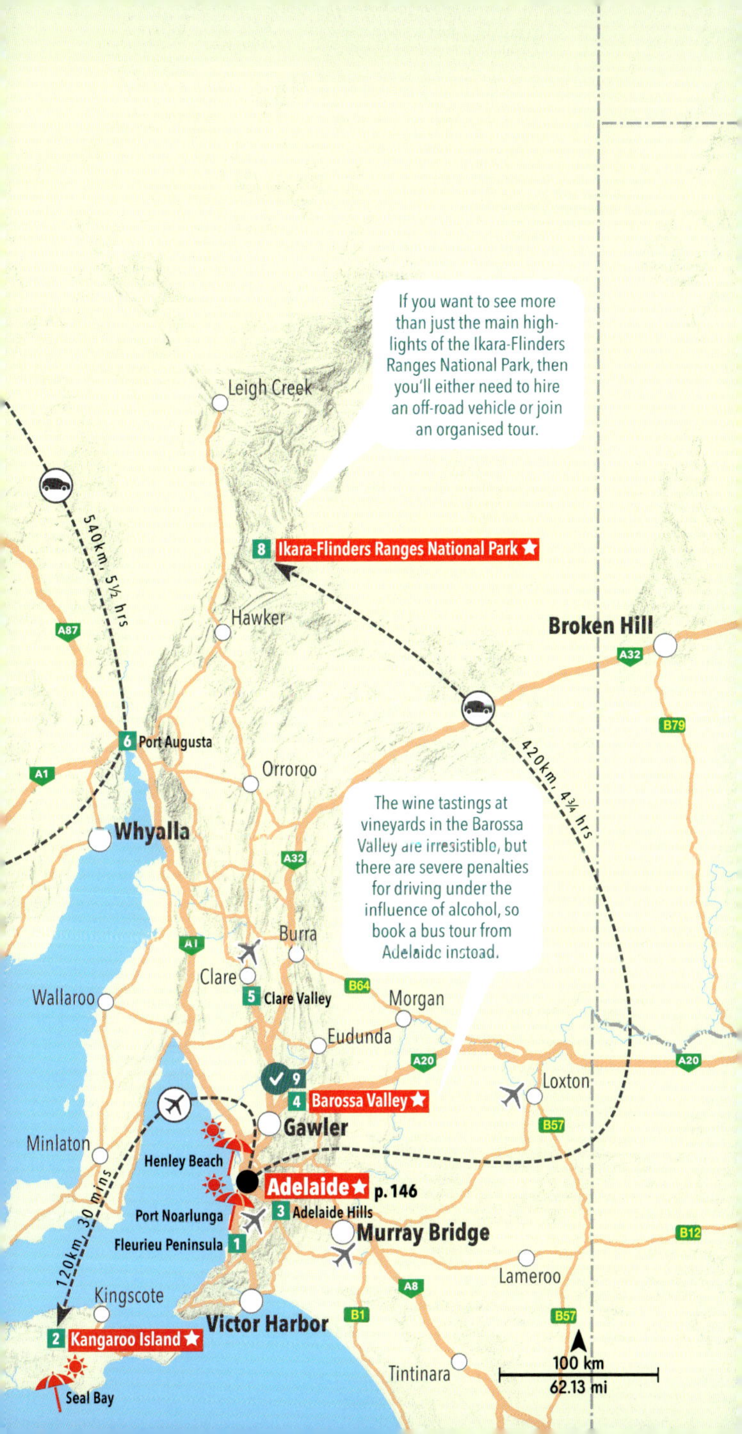

If you want to see more than just the main highlights of the Ikara-Flinders Ranges National Park, then you'll either need to hire an off-road vehicle or join an organised tour.
Leigh Creek
540km, 5½ hrs
8 Ikara-Flinders Ranges National Park
Hawker
Broken Hill
A87
A32
6 Port Augusta
B79
A1
Orroroo
420km, 4¾ hrs
Whyalla
The wine tastings at vineyards in the Barossa Valley are irresistible, but there are severe penalties for driving under the influence of alcohol, so book a bus tour from Adelaide instead.
A32
Burra
A1
Clare
B64
5 Clare Valley
Wallaroo
Morgan
Eudunda
A20
A20
9
4 Barossa Valley
Loxton
Gawler
B57
Minlaton
Henley Beach
Adelaide p.146
3 Adelaide Hills
Port Noarlunga
Murray Bridge
B12
Fleurieu Peninsula 1
120km, 30 mins
Lameroo
Kingscote
A8
Victor Harbor
B1
B57
2 Kangaroo Island
100 km
62.13 mi
Tintinara
Seal Bay

ADELAIDE

(📖 F6) **Year after year, ★ Adelaide (pop. 1.4 million) safely secures a spot in the list of the world's top ten most liveable cities.**

WHERE TO START?

Victoria Square is a good starting point if you fancy something to eat in a Grote Street restaurant or want to take the tram to Glenelg. It's a ten-minute walk to **North Terrace**, the first address for the city's main attractions. And if you arrive by train, the railway station is also on North Terrace.

The city and its parks may have a certain tranquil charm, but venture out to coastal suburbs like Brighton, Glenelg or Henley Beach, or take a trip to the Adelaide Hills and the wine regions of Barossa Valley and McLaren Vale, and there's no doubt about it: life here is pretty sweet.

Just so you know, no convicts came to South Australia – a fact South Australians are keen to point out. Many of the European settlers who arrived in the first half of the 19th century were people who had to leave their native countries for religious or political reasons. Adelaide is still a tolerant, multicultural and cultivated city with numerous museums, theatres and concert halls.

The 🐷 *Adelaide Greeters (tel. 13 00 58 81 40 | short.travel/aus25)* will be delighted to guide you around the city free of charge. Not only is this a great way to glean some background info, you might even make a new friend. Make sure to book at least three days in advance!

SIGHTSEEING

ART GALLERY OF SOUTH AUSTRALIA

A must for art lovers: with 35,000 works of art, the museum houses the second-biggest art collection in Australia. The Australian collection is particularly impressive. *Daily 10am–5pm | admission free | North Terrace | agsa.sa.gov.au | 1–2 hrs*

SOUTH AUSTRALIAN MUSEUM

The longest snake – the wonambi – measures 6m from tip to tail, and crushes its prey to death. Thankfully, it has been extinct for around 40,000 years. You'll only encounter this representative of Australia's megafauna here at the museum – or rather, the fossil of one. Be sure to visit the Australian Aboriginal cultures gallery too. *Daily 10am–5pm | admission free | North Terrace | samuseum.sa.gov.au | 1 ½ hrs*

MIGRATION MUSEUM

Did you know that German immigrants were instrumental in shaping Adelaide? Step into their shoes for an hour or two at the museum. *Daily 10am–5pm | admission free (donations welcome) | 82 Kintore Av | migration.history.sa.gov.au | 1 ½ hrs*

TANDANYA – NATIONAL ABORIGINAL CULTURAL INSTITUTE

The cultural institute of the Kuarna people has art and craft galleries and changing exhibitions. There are often good *cultural performances* during the school holidays; information online. *Mon–Sat 10am–5pm | admission free | 253 Grenfell Street | tel. 08 82 24 32 00 | tandanya.com.au | 1 hr*

ADELAIDE BOTANIC GARDEN

You might have spotted the large, eye-catching glass building when you approached Adelaide on the flight in. The greenhouse with brightly coloured birds and insects is only one of the highlights in this peaceful park. *Mon–Fri 7.15am–sunset, Sat/Sun from 9am, free guided tours daily 10.30am from Schomburgk Pavilion | admission free | North Terrace | botanicgardens.sa.gov.au | 1–2 hrs*

NATIONAL WINE CENTRE

The futuristic Wine Centre building is on the edge of the Botanic Garden. Interactive displays tell you everything you want to know about the cultivation, care and harvesting of the wines of South Australia. The region is especially well known for its earthy, spicy reds. The centre has an excellent cellar where rare Australian wines can also be bought. *Wine tastings, set menus & tours | Yarrabee House, Botanic Rd/Hackney Rd | from A$25 | nationalwinecentre.com.au | 1–2 hrs*

GLENELG

The tram from Victoria Square to the most popular beach suburb in Adelaide takes about 20 minutes. Browse the shops on Jetty Road, grab an ice cream and stroll out onto the jetty. Catamarans run by *Temptation Sailing* leave from Holdfast Marina, just five minutes from the tram stop, for "swim with dolphins" tours *(3½-hr tour from A$149, watching from A$88 | tel. 04 12 81 18 38 | dolphinboat.com.au)*.

INSIDER TIP
Swim with dolphins

MOUNT LOFTY

This viewpoint will give you a sense of the city's beautiful setting, amid lush parkland with the sea close at hand. Enjoy the panoramic views and natural surroundings on the 1km *Discovery Walk*, or climb to the summit from the car park in *Waterfall Gully (4.5km)*. Refreshments are available from the *Summit Cafe (Mon–Fri 9am–4pm, Sat/Sun 8am–4.30pm | mountloftysummit.com)*.

CLELAND WILDLIFE PARK

Feed kangaroos and emus against the backdrop of the Adelaide skyline. This large park is the perfect chance to get up close and personal with the local wildlife. Animal feed is sold at the entrance. *Daily 9.30am–5pm | A$34, children A$18, families A$83 | 365 Mount Lofty Summit Rd, Crafters | clelandwildlifepark.sa.gov.au | 1 ½ hrs*

EATING & DRINKING

The *Central Market* and neighbouring *Gouger Street* have the biggest selection of restaurants and cafés.

JASMIN INDIAN RESTAURANT

The scent of cumin, cardamom and nutmeg alone will make your mouth water. *Tue–Sat dinner, also lunch Thu/Fri | 31 Hindmarsh Sq | tel. 08 82 23 78 37 | jasmin.com.au | $$*

RED OCHRE

Kangaroo steak and Australian shellfish: venture into new culinary territory at this local restaurant, whose menu is inspired by Indigenous cuisine. If you can't decide what to have, then try the six-course "Feed me" menu *(A$85/pers)*. *Thu–Sat from 6pm | War Memorial Drive | tel. 08 82 11 85 55 | redochrebarrelandgrill.com.au | $$$*

INSIDER TIP
Tasting menu

SHOPPING

Adelaide is good for opals, outback clothing, craft items and local art. *Rundle Mall* is the main shopping centre, with shops, cafés and arcades, and the often-photographed bronze pigs. Also good are *King William Road (Hyde Park | kingwilliamroad.com.au)* and the *Jam Factory Contemporary Craft & Design (19 Morphett St | jamfactory.com.au)*.

CENTRAL MARKET

The covered market has more than 80 stands with vegetables, fruit, fish and meat from the area. Asian and

European dishes can be sampled at small stands. *Tue–Sat | Grote St | adelaidecentralmarket.com.au*

BEACHES

Beautiful sandy beaches stretch along the entire coastline. The first ports of call from the city are *Glenelg* and *Henley Beach*. Carry on south for other great beaches: enjoy the view from the esplanade in *Brighton*, snorkel the reef in *Port Noarlunga* and ride the waves in *Moana*, which is particularly popular with surfers.

NIGHTLIFE

What's on in Adelaide (whatsonin adelaide.net.au) knows what's going on where in the city. Tickets for many events can be booked through the *Adelaide Festival Centre (tel. 13 12 46 | adelaidefestivalcentre.com.au)*. The most popular live music venues are *Hindley Street Music Hall (145 Hindley Street | hindleymusichall.com.au)* and *The Gov (59 Port Rd, Hindmarsh | thegov.com.au)*. Other cultural offerings can be found on *songkick.com*.

AROUND ADELAIDE

1 FLEURIEU PENINSULA

50km / 1 hr from Adelaide by car

This peninsula located to the south is where the people of Adelaide gather at weekends for wine tastings, coastal hikes or snorkelling in secluded coves.

Inland, around rural *McLaren Vale (mclarenvale.info)*, there are more than a hundred wineries. In this

Adelaide Arcade is part of the Rundle Mall

renowned wine-growing region, live music, open-air cinema and food trucks are often on offer. At the *d'Arenberg Cube (daily 10.30am–4.30pm | A$20 | 58 Osborn Rd, McLaren Vale | ⏲ 2 hrs)*, which looks like a Rubik's Cube, you can work your way through the museum floors to the observation deck, where you can do wine tasting.

Goolwa on *Lake Alexandrina* is popular. It has a lovely beach, lots of restaurants and places to stay and dine. From here you can explore the *Coorong National Park* on a boat trip; *Spirit of the Coorong (from A$165 | tel. 08 85 55 22 03 | spiritofthecoorong.com.au)*.

In cosy *Victor Harbor (visitvictorharbor.com)* (pop. 16,000), pop into the *South Australian Whale Centre (daily 10am–4pm | A$5 | 2 Railway Terraces | sawhalecentre.com.au | ⏲ 1½ hrs)*. It provides information on the southern right whales that can be seen here between June and September. *Granite Island* off Victor Harbor is home to around 2,000 tiny fairy penguins and can be reached across a wooden bridge on foot or on the historical horse-drawn tram *(daily 10am–4pm | return ticket A$25 | horsedrawntram.com.au)*. *F6*.

2 KANGAROO ISLAND ★

120km / 30 mins from Adelaide by plane

Kangaroo Island is an example of just how resilient the Australian natural world is. This paradise for animal- and nature-lovers just off the coast of Adelaide made tragic headlines in early 2020 when virtually the entire western half of the island was ravaged by bushfires. Countless animals, including koalas and kangaroos, lost their lives, and infrastructure and homes were reduced to rubble. But not for long. Soon bright green buds were sprouting from the pitch-blackened tree trunks, and today the trees are once again filled with bird-song and rustling sounds.

More than 30 per cent of the bush-land is a national park. Huge colonies of seals and sea lions occupy the island's beaches. Accompanied by rangers, a colony of several hundred sea lions can be visited in *Seal Bay Conservation Park (guided tours daily from 9am | from A$42)* on *Seal Bay* in the south. In the evenings, pelicans crowd around the pier in *Kingscote*. In the winter, southern right whales rest out at sea.

Those who want even more than hiking or animal-watching can swim, surf, dive, ride and cycle on Kangaroo Island. You can also stock up on honey and eucalyptus oil products – and eat very well too. Call in at *Island Beehive (59 Playford Highway, Kingscote)* and sample their exquisite Stringy Bark honey to really excite your tastebuds.

INSIDER TIP Honey tasting

You can reach the island from Cape Jervis on the Fleurieu Peninsula via the *Kangaroo Island Sealink Ferry (car and 2 pers A$472 return | tel. 013 13 01 | sealink.com.au)* to Penneshaw in just under a hour. There is no public transport on the island, but you can hire a car from *Thrifty (from A$95/day |*

The vines in the Barossa Valley have German roots

Thomas Wilson St, Penneshaw | tel. 13 00 11 01 96 | thrifty.com.au). Island tours are available through *Exceptional Kangaroo Island (day tour A$600 | tel. 08 85 53 91 19 | exceptionalkangarooisland.com)*. *tourkangarooisland.com.au* | F6–7

3 ADELAIDE HILLS

27km / 35 mins from Adelaide by car

The gently rolling landscape of the Adelaide Hills starts some 27km from Adelaide. Fifty Lutheran migrant families who arrived in South Australia aboard the ship *Zebra* founded the village of *Hahndorf* (pop. 3,100) in 1839. Half-timbered, German-style houses, an old German butcher's, a German inn, an antique clock museum and numerous souvenir shops and restaurants attract tourists to Hahndorf. *adelaidehills.org.au* | F6

4 BAROSSA VALLEY ★

73km / 1 hr from Adelaide by car

Excellent wines, rye bread, sourdough, cheese, olives, smoked sausages and ham – and historical villages in pretty countryside: that's "The Barossa", northeast of Adelaide and a must for wine-lovers because it has more than 150 wineries. The first British farmers settled here in 1840. They were joined in 1842 by Lutherans from Silesia, Brandenburg and Poznan, who brought the first vines to the now world-famous wine-growing area.

The German settlement of *Bethany* is a traditional elongated village with houses on one side of the road and small fields on the other. *Tanunda* (pop. 4,700), formerly Langmeil, is a good starting point for a wine and gourmet tour through the region. It's a good idea to stay at least one night here in one of the many beautiful B&Bs offering vineyard views and sumptuous breakfasts. From the *Barossa Visitor Centre (66–68 Murray St, Tanunda | tel. 13 00 85 29 82 | barossa.com)* you can pick up the *Winery Map* with a description of *Scenic Drive 4* through the Barossa Valley. It is well worth stopping at the wineries on Para Road as well as at Penfolds, Charles Melton, Bethany Wines and Villa Tinto. The vast *Seppeltsfield Winery* has created its very own "archive": since 1878, a barrel of every vintage has been stored there and you can taste wine from your birth year *(A$109 incl. tour)*. F6

5 CLARE VALLEY

140km / 2 hrs from Adelaide by car

North of Adelaide lies another idyllic wine-growing region. It's worth spending a couple of days here, especially if you want to visit one or two of the award-winning wineries. *Knappstein Wines (daily 10am–4pm, Fri until 7pm | 2 Pioneer Av | knappstein.com.au)* sets the standard for the very best-quality wines, both red and white. At *Skillogalee Wines (daily 9.30am–5pm | skillogalee.com.au)*, you don't just get served a light Riesling to drink but also a delicious lunch. Those with at least one more day to spare can explore the wine-growing area between *Auburn* and *Clare* by bike along the *Riesling Trail*. Bikes can be hired from *Clare Valley Cycle Hire (56 Warenda Rd | 04 75 73 37 47 | clarevalleycyclehire.com.au)*, while further information is available from the *Clare Valley Wine, Food & Tourism Centre (8 Spring Gully Rd | tel. 18 00 24 21 31 | clarevalley.com.au)*. F6

INSIDER TIP
Wine on two wheels

6 PORT AUGUSTA

305km / 3½ hrs from Adelaide by car

The harbour town (pop. 14,000) with a charming historical centre is primarily a supply centre for the remote interior further north. It is a gateway to the outback, both by road and rail: the Stuart Highway and legendary "Ghan" train service go from here to Darwin, and the Eyre Highway ends in Western Australia. An excellent insight into the outback and its extensive history is available at the *Wadlata Outback Centre (Mon–Fri 9am–4pm, Sat/Sun 10am–3pm | A$22 | 41 Flinders Terrace | wadlata.sa.gov.au | 1½ hrs)*. F6

7 EYRE PENINSULA ★

638km / 7 hrs from Adelaide by car

A wonderful coastline with fine sandy beaches is the trademark of this peninsula west of Adelaide. The desert plains and outback of the Gawler Ranges and the dried-up salt lake *Lake Gairdner* can be found further inland. Kangaluna Camp, a comfortable campsite, is at the centre. From here, it is around a two-hour drive to *Baird Bay*. This beautiful bay is the perfect spot to swim with sea lions and dolphins *(daily from 9am | A$325 | bairdbay.com)*, and these curious sea creatures are usually happy to get nose to nose. Why not make a detour to Talia Cave and the gorgeous beach at Venus Bay? *E–F6*

INSIDER TIP
Face to face with a sea lion

8 IKARA-FLINDERS RANGES NATIONAL PARK ★

420km / 4¾ hrs from Adelaide by car

The bizarre rock formations that shimmer in reds and violets above the expanse of the plain more than 400km north of Adelaide make up this national park that covers 950km². Deep gorges cut through this largely arid region. Most tours and places to stay in this fantastic wilderness have to be booked beforehand in Adelaide. A 4WD car is only needed if you intend to leave the main route. *Wilpena Pound*, a huge area surrounded by jagged rocks, is the most characteristic landmark of the Flinders Ranges. You can hike around this natural amphitheatre, known as the Cauldron, in a day (approx. 20km, 9 hours). St Mary Peak is a sacred site for the Indigenous people, so please refrain from making the detour to the summit. Over 500 million years ago, this high plateau was at the bottom of the sea, as is confirmed by the countless fossils in the rocks.

For accommodation, the *Wilpena Pound Resort (wilpenapound.com.au)* is a good choice and provides maps and information.

Rock paintings in the Flinders Ranges provide evidence of prehistoric lives in the region

Iga Warta (tel. 08 86 48 37 37 | igawarta.com) is a cultural centre that introduces visitors to the culture of the Adnyamathanha people. Indigenous guides show guests some of the many rock paintings and engravings in the gorges of the Flinders Ranges. Guests help hunt and collect bush food, hike or ride out on horses into the heart of the mountains. Tours *(from A$75)* can last from just a few hours to several days. If you want to stay, pitch your tent on Iga Warta (near Copley), or book one of the rustic cabins or safari tents. *F5–6*

COOBER PEDY

(E5) **Raging heat by day, frost at night. And flies! The climate at Coober Pedy (pop. 1,600), halfway between Adelaide and Alice Springs, is so difficult that the whole town virtually lives underground. So why on earth would anyone even want to make this their home?**

Simple: around three-quarters of the world's white opals are found in and around Coober Pedy (from the Kokatha term *kuba piti* for "white man in a hole"). With daytime temperatures of up to 45°C and icy cold at night, it's not surprising that most people live in disused mines. Entire homes and even churches and hotels have been bored into the hillsides. The temperature in the "dugouts" is a pleasant 24°C all year round.

A good insight into life here and the nature of the outback is provided on the *Mail Run (Mon & Thu 9am | 600km in about 12 hrs | approx. A$350 | tel. 04 18 31 43 71 | mailrun tour.com.au)*, which goes from Coober Pedy to *Oodnadatta* and *William Creek*.

The destination of an hour-long sightseeing flight is *Anna Creek Painted Hills*, a 300km² rocky outcrop of large and small hills that shimmer in all colours *(half-day tour from Coober Pedy or William Creek | A$450 | wrightsair.com.au)*.

SIGHTSEEING

OLD TIMERS MINE

Tours are run to these former opal mines. Two dugout houses can also be visited. *Daily 9am–5pm | A$15 | Crowders Gully Road | oldtimersmine.com.au*

EATING & DRINKING

OUTBACK BAR & GRILL

Service station, pub and restaurant in one. It might not sound inviting, but the burgers are the best in town. *Daily | 454 Hutchison St | tel. 08 86 72 32 50 | $*

SHOPPING

Shops in Hutchison Street work opals and sell jewellery. Prices here are lower than in cities *(cooberpedy.com/opals-2)*. Check out *Opalios (8 Hutchison St | opalios.com.au)*, for example.

Life in a dugout in Coober Pedy

AROUND COOBER PEDY

9 KANKU BREAKAWAYS CONSERVATION PARK

32km / ½ hr from Coober Pedy by car

The hilly, sparsely vegetated area that glows in different colours depending on the position of the sun is north of Coober Pedy and is a popular film location. Panorama Hill, for example, played an important role in the action film *Mad Max*, which helped Mel Gibson to his international breakthrough in 1979. *Admission A$10 | permits: Coober Pedy Visitor Information Centre, Hutchison St |* *E5*

SLEEP WELL IN SOUTH AUSTRALIA

FIRE STATION OR VILLA?

The *North Adelaide Heritage Group (tel. 08 82 67 20 20 | adelaide heritage.com | $$$)* offers 19 different accommodation options in central and north Adelaide in historical properties. Make yourself at home in Adelaide's very first fire station or treat yourself to a stay in an old mansion.

GOING UNDERGROUND

Find out what it's like to live in a dugout at *The Underground Motel (9 rooms | Catacomb Rd, Coober Pedy | tel. 08 86 72 53 24 | the undergroundmotel.com.au | $$)*. Opened in 1984, this was the country's first subterranean hotel. Today the rooms have fresh-air vents and even a little bit of sunlight.

TASMANIA

AUSTRALIA'S ISLAND STATE

To the rest of the country, Tasmania is that little island "under Down Under" where time somehow passes more slowly. Tasmanians, for their part, confidently call the Australian mainland "the North Island".

Despite its compact size, Tasmania has a lot to offer: almost one-third of its countryside is a protected area – craggy mountain peaks, huge ferns, giant trees covered with moss, fast-flowing streams, lakes and hidden beaches. Then there are the stunning

Dove Lake and Cradle Mountain

mountain landscapes inland, edged by divine bays along the east coast.

Cut off from mainland Australia, plants and animals have evolved here that cannot be found anywhere else. The main island is about three times the size of Wales and is the smallest and coldest state in Australia. Most of the 520,000 or so inhabitants live in Hobart in the south and Launceston in the north. Tasmania can best be explored by hire car. In summer, accommodation should be booked in advance.

TASMANIA

MARCO POLO BUCKET LIST

10 ✓ Hike to the end of the world

Experience the wilderness of the Tasman Peninsula on the *Three Capes Track* ➤ p. 162

The Overland Track through Cradle Mountain-Lake St Clair National Park is breath-taking … and almost always over-subscribed. Book your place well in advance!

MARCO POLO HIGHLIGHTS

★ HOBART
The Tasmanian capital enjoys a perfect mix of mountains and coast ➤ p. 160

★ PORT ARTHUR
Ruins with a gruesome past, surrounded by delightful scenery ➤ p. 162

★ FREYCINET NATIONAL PARK
Queen Elizabeth II herself soaked up the view at Wineglass Bay with its secluded beaches ➤ p. 165

★ CRADLE MOUNTAIN-LAKE ST CLAIR NATIONAL PARK
Virtually untouched mountain landscapes with superb hiking trails ➤ p. 167

★ STRAHAN
Fishing village that is the gateway to Tasmania's wilderness ➤ p. 168

★ FRANKLIN-GORDON WILD RIVERS NATIONAL PARK
Jungle expedition by boat ➤ p. 169

You can do your bit for the conservation of the endangered Tasmanian devil by moving roadkill from the highway into the verge (only if it's safe to do so, of course!). Carrion provides easy pickings for Tasmanian devils but often results in them becoming roadkill themselves.
Bridport
180km, 2¾ hrs
Scottsdale
5 Beauty Point
A3
6 Bay of Fires
Exeter
4 Hollybank Treetop Adventure
St. Helens
p. 165
Georges Bay
Launceston
p. 163
Deloraine
Evandale
Longford
St Marys
Fingal
A4
1
TASMANIA
Bicheno
Campbell Town
200km, 2½ hrs
Swansea
Wineglass Bay
8 Freycinet National Park
A5
Oatlands
Bothwell
If you're travelling along the east coast of Tasmania, make an excursion to Maria Island; boats depart from Triabunna.
A3
1
Orford
7 Maria Island
Brighton
Sorell
New Norfolk
nanyi (Mount Wellington) 1
Hobart
p. 160
Summer is the best time to visit Hobart, when the calendar is packed with events. However, this is also the school holidays, so book accommodation and activities well in advance.
Huonville
Kingston
Tasman Peninsula 3
Port Arthur
Nubeena
10
A6
Dover
Adventure Bay
Bruny Island 2
50 km
31 mi

HOBART

(📖 H8) **Mountains, bush and bays: romantic ★ Hobart (pop. 252,000), with its well-preserved colonial buildings, nestles among spectacular mountains at the mouth of the deep-blue Derwent River.**

The centre of activity is the unbelievably pretty natural harbour of *Sullivans Cove*. On a clear day, the views from *Mount Wellington* are beyond compare.

WHERE TO START?

Sullivans Cove, where tourist boats and ferries come in, is a good place to start a stroll around the city centre and the historical districts of Salamanca Place and Battery Point. If you arrive by bus, get off at Franklin Square/Elizabeth Street, not far from the travel centre.

SIGHTSEEING

BATTERY POINT

Tiny traditional workers' houses with front gardens full of flowers, old sandstone villas, independent cafés, bookshops and antique shops are features of Hobart's oldest area, around Hampden Road. Climb the old stone Kellys Steps from Salamanca Place to Battery Point and stroll to Arthurs Circus, the old village square. Hampden Road has some lovely cafés as well as the small 🐖 *Narryna Heritage Museum (Tue–Sat 10am–4pm, daily in summer | admission free | narrnya.com.au | ⏲ ½ hr).*

Take a break for coffee and baked goodies at Jackman & McRoss

MONA (MUSEUM OF OLD AND NEW ART)

A machine that digests food like a human body and 150 reproductions of the female reproductive organs – in porcelain. Call that art? This private collection belonging to an eccentric multi-millionaire is as famous as it is provocative. And it has catapulted Hobart onto the world's modern art stage.

The complex also includes a brewery, *Moo Brew*, a wine cellar and bar, and an elegant restaurant, *The Source (Thu–Mon noon–4pm | $$$)*. You can also get there by boat *(from Brook St Ferry Terminal/Sullivans Cove). Thu–Mon 10am–5pm | A$39 | 655 Main Rd, Berriedale | mona.net.au | 2 hrs*

EATING & DRINKING

BLUE EYE

Small restaurant serving fresh seafood. Enjoy Tasmanian wines and a view out over the hustle and bustle of Salamanca Place. *Daily | Castray Esplanade/Salamanca Place | tel. 03 62 23 52 97 | blueeye.net.au | $$$*

FISH FRENZY

An institution which always serves wonderfully fresh seafood. *Daily | Elizabeth Street Pier | tel. 03 62 31 21 34 | fishfrenzy.com.au | $$–$$$*

JACKMAN & MCROSS

This bustling bakery is great for a coffee break or breakfast. *57 Hampden Rd | Battery Point*

MURES

This restaurant has its own fleet of fishing boats. Guests can choose between the elegant dining room on the first floor *($$–$$$)*, a self-service area on the ground floor *($–$$)* and a sushi bar *($$–$$$). Daily | Victoria Dock, Sullivans Cove | tel. 03 62 31 20 09 | mures.com.au*

SPORT & ACTIVITIES

Premier Travel Tasmania (tel. 03 62 31 42 14 | premiertraveltasmania.com) organises very good tours lasting one or several days *(from A$355)* for groups of two or more people, with a special emphasis on watching wildlife and exploring the natural beauty of Tasmania.

NIGHTLIFE

Late in the afternoon on Fridays, you can enjoy live music at *Rektango (5.30–7.30pm)* in the courtyard of historical Salamanca Place – absolutely free of charge.

AROUND HOBART

1 KUNANYI (MOUNT WELLINGTON)

17km / 25 mins from Hobart by car

Make sure to take a jacket, because a cold wind can blow up here even on summer days. Going "up" is a must, because the view over Hobart – and on a clear day even as far Bruny Island – is simply unbeatable. You can drive to the top. If you prefer to hike, take the two- to three-hour *Organ Pipes Walk*, which leads from The Springs to the giant stone pillars dotted along the route. H8

INSIDER TIP
Organ pipes in the mountains

2 BRUNY ISLAND

70km / 1½ hrs from Hobart to Adventure Bay by car and ferry

Perhaps you've already spied it from the top of Mount Wellington: Bruny Island, ringed by white sand. it is, in fact, two islands: North Bruny and South Bruny, joined by a narrow isthmus known as "The Neck". A visit is highly recommended. Climb the steep steps to the *Truganini Lookout*, ideally around sunrise or sunset when little penguins waddle from their nests to the sea.

You'll get an end-of-the-world feeling in the *South Bruny National Park (Park Pass A$46.60/car | short.travel/aus65)*, where the sea crashes into rugged rocks. On a clear day, the view from the *Cape Bruny Lighthouse (tour A$25 | capebrunylighthouse.com)* stretches as far as the South East Cape, the southernmost point of Australia. H8

3 TASMAN PENINSULA

100km / 1½ hrs from Hobart by car

Even a glance at the map will tell you that this is a special piece of land. The peninsula hangs off Tasmania like a ripe fruit at the end of a stalk, as though it could drop off and drift away into the ocean at any moment. Little wonder that the country's colonial masters once thought they'd found the perfect prison and shipped the worst crooks and criminals here. The causeway to the mainland was guarded by dogs, and anyone who attempted to escape by sea had to contend with shark-infested waters.

Thus, in the 1830s, ★ *Port Arthur*, the most notorious penal facility in Australia, was established on this remote outpost. Visiting the ruins of the prison will give you goosebumps to this day, especially if you join one of the guided tours *(daily 9am–5pm | from A$48 incl. Harbour Cruise | portarthur.org.au)*. Tickets are valid for two days so that you've plenty of time to explore the site. In the evening, a 90-minute *Ghost Tour (A$35)* reveals the resident ghosts.

Around 10km from Port Arthur, at the Koonya turn-off, is the *Tasmanian Devil Unzoo (daily 9am–5pm | A$55 | Port Arthur Highway, Taranna | tasmaniandevilunzoo.com.au | 1½ hrs)*, where you can find out about the endangered marsupial.

The peninsula's coastline is so dramatic that you'll want to pull on your walking boots straightaway. The highlights are the three capes: *Cape Raoul* and *Cape Hauy* can each be reached on a half-day hike, whereas you'll have to factor in a night under canvas to get to *Cape Pillar*. The four-day *Three Capes Track (A$615 | reservations required | threecapestrack.com.au)* links Port Arthur with two of the capes (a separate tour heads to Cape Raoul) and includes accommodation in comfortable huts along the route.

Instead of a boat trip through the Cataract Gorge, cross the Alexandra Suspension Bridge

The rock needles and columns at Cape Hauy, which reach up to 60m above sea level, are a designated climbing location and are especially impressive when seen from the water. *Tasman Island Cruises (from A$180 | tel. 03 62 50 22 00 | tasmancruises.com.au)* offer three-hour boat trips along the coast from Port Arthur, including a visit to the seal colony. Take a sea-sickness tablet before departure; the boat tends to pitch a lot! *H8*

LAUNCESTON

(H8) **Tasmania's second largest city (pop. 91,000) is a very popular gourmet destination.**

You don't just get to visit the many good restaurants but also the vineyards and fruit plantations in nearby Tamar Valley. Numerous historical buildings and parks can be found in Launceston city centre.

SIGHTSEEING

CATARACT GORGE

The deep gorge of the fast-flowing *South Esk River* reaches right into the heart of the city. A walk that lasts around one hour takes you across the swaying Alexandra suspension bridge up to the steep *Eagle Eyrie Lookout* and on to the old *Toll House on Kings Bridge*. A one-hour boat trip with *Tamar River Cruises (daily 9.30am–3.30pm | from A$40 | Home Point*

Wineglass Bay

Cruise Terminal, at the end of Home Point Parade | tel. 03 63 34 99 00 | tamarrivercruises.com.au) through the dramatic rocky gorge is equally enticing.

EATING & DRINKING

PIPER'S BROOK VINEYARD

Lunch surrounded by vineyards can be enjoyed in a number of wineries north of Launceston. Piper's Brook Vineyard has great food and lovely views from the terrace. *Daily 10am–4pm | 1216 Pipers Brook Rd | kreglingerwineestates.com | $-$$*

STILLWATER

This trendy bistro serves award-winning cuisine. *Daily | 2 Bridge Rd | tel. 03 63 31 41 53 | $$$*

THREE STEPS ON GORGE

Australian pub classics like steak or fish and chips are on the menu at this old hotel. Live music often adds to the great atmosphere. *Daily | 158 Gorge St | tel. 03 63 34 20 84 | $$*

AROUND LAUNCESTON

4 HOLLYBANK TREETOP ADVENTURE

20km / 20 mins from Launceston by car

This adrenalin-kick zip-line adventure at a dizzying height is undiluted, action-packed, outdoor fun. Attached to ropes, participants "fly" over distances of up to 370m. You can even take a trip in the dark on a "night flight". *Daily 9am–5pm | 3 hrs incl. briefing approx. A$100 | 66 Hollybank Rd, Underwood | treetopsadventure.com.au |* H8

INSIDER TIP
Zip along

5 BEAUTY POINT

50km / ¾ hr from Launceston by car

Three attractions await day trippers here on the western bank of the Tamar River, which is quite wide at this point. At the *Platypus House (daily 9.30am–4pm | A$30 | platypushouse.com.au | 2 hrs)*, you can also see the shy echidna, and at neighbouring *Seahorse World (daily 9.30am–4pm | A$28 | seahorseworld.com.au | 1½ hrs)* you can observe these tiny little creatures up close. To the southwest at *Beaconsfield*, the *Mine and Heritage Centre (daily 10am–4pm | A$20 | West St | beaconsfield heritage.com.au | 1 hr)* offers exciting insights into the history of Tasmania's biggest goldmine. *H8*

ST HELENS

(H8) **This former whaling station in the east (pop. 2,200) has become a lively holiday resort centred around sheltered Georges Bay.**

There is a good selection of accommodation and restaurants, plus the tranquil bay, where you can swim safely.

AROUND ST HELENS

6 BAY OF FIRES

27km / 40 mins from St Helens by car

This elongated bay to the north has fabulous, secluded, snowy-white beaches. En route, be sure to turn off to *Binalong Bay (binalongbay.com.au)* to understand where the bay gets its name: thanks to a dense layer of lichen, the granite rocks glow fiery red. Some wildly romantic campsites offer accommodation right beside the sea, although there is no electricity. *H8*

7 MARIA ISLAND

170km / 2¾ hrs from St Helens by car and ferry

For a short time, Maria Island served as a penal facility, but its proximity to the mainland meant that it wasn't considered secure enough. Nevertheless, the island was secluded enough to become a natural refuge for wildlife: kangaroos, wallabies, wombats, geese and countless other birds live here, alongside a small number of Tasmanian devils that have been brought here in the last few years to protect them from the contagious, malignant Tasmanian devil facial tumour disease.

Wander among the historical buildings of the former settlement of *Darlington* and hike to the *Painted Cliffs* on the west coast *(about a 90-min round trip from Darlington)*. There are no motorised vehicles on the island, but you can hire a bike from the boat jetty on arrival *(A$40/day | encountermaria.com.au/bike-hire)*.

You can reach Maria Island by ferry from *Triabunna (30 mins | Sept–April daily, May–Aug Fri–Mon, Wed | A$55 return | encountermaria.com.au)*. The boat trips with *East Coast Cruises (day trip incl. food and drink A$290 | eastcoastcruises.com.au)* are highly recommended; you'll learn the exciting history of the island while on board. *H8*

8 FREYCINET NATIONAL PARK ★

120km / 1½ hrs from St Helens by car

Protected countryside with secluded sandy beaches – the one in *Wineglass Bay* is considered one of the loveliest in the world, and it's most certainly worth the approximately three-hour walk from the car park and back.

There are wonderful views of the coast from the water, either on a five-hour *Eco Cruise (from A$175 | tel. 03 62 57 03 55 | wineglassbaycruises.com.au)* in a sleek catamaran, or – if you want something a little sportier and to paddle yourself – in a kayak from *Freycinet Adventures (A$145) | tel. 03 62 57 05 00 | freycinetadventures.com.au).* H8

DEVONPORT

(H8) **Devonport (pop. 26,000) is the gateway to Tasmania's rugged northwest.**

Daily car ferries from Melbourne dock in the town's port. From Mersey Bluff, with its lighthouse, you get a spectacular view along the coast as far as Burnie on a clear day.

EATING & DRINKING

MRS JONES RESTAURANT

Dishes on the international menu are prepared using fresh local ingredients and are served on the top floor of the surf club with views of the water. Do try the tempura oysters! *Closed Mon/Tue | Williams St/corner Bluff Rd | tel. 03 64 23 38 81 | mrsjonesrbl.com.au | $$$*

AROUND DEVONPORT

9 DELORAINE

54km / 40 mins from Devonport by car

For gourmets, this rural town to the southeast is well worth a detour. The salmon farm *41° South (6km further southwest | signposted on the Montana Road | 41southtasmania.com)*, farms this delicious fish without using any chemicals. The small shop sells fresh salmon, smoked products and salmon paste. And if you fancy something sweet, head for *Honey Farm (39 Sorell St | approx. 20km west, in Chudleigh | melitahoneyfarm.com.au)*. The star among the many types of honey is the aromatic *leatherwood honey* from the pollen of local giant trees. H8

10 STANLEY

125km / 1½ hrs from Devonport by car

Victorian houses and small shops line the old main street in Stanley (pop. 600) below *The Nut (Circular Head)*. The steep rock is a popular place for sightseers. The hike up takes 10–20 minutes, and you'll be rewarded with a lovely circular walk (approx. 30 mins) around the top. A little easier and just as scenic is the chairlift *(daily 9.30am–4.15pm | return A$21 | thenutchairlift.com.au)*.

Penguins and colonies of sea lions can be visited on the coast, or take a boat trip *(75 mins | A$55 | tel. 03 64 58 12 94 | stanleysealcruises.com.au)*.

You'll find it hard to leave the beautiful surroundings of Cradle Mountain Lodge

If you're feeling peckish, *Stanley's Hotel (daily | 15 Wharf Rd | tel. 03 64 58 11 61 | stanleyvillage.com.au | $$)* is an excellent restaurant with a lovely rooftop terrace where you can enjoy local delicacies. *(map) G8*

CRADLE MOUNTAIN-LAKE ST CLAIR NP

(map G8) **Tasmania is a destination for hiking boots, not car tyres. The highlight is ★ Cradle Mountain-Lake St Clair National Park, which is nestled between tranquil mountain lakes and rugged peaks.**

Lake St Clair in the south boasts a romantic and peaceful shoreline. Meanwhile, thanks to its tourist infrastructure, Cradle Valley in the north has become a kind of central hub for the national park. From here, a shuttle service takes hikers to the start of numerous trails. You'll need to purchase a park pass *(A$29/pers or A$47/car incl. shuttle service)*.

EATING & DRINKING

HIGHLAND RESTAURANT

This renowned restaurant, complete with wood-burning stove, is as rustic as it is chic. Plus, it's part of the comfortable *Cradle Mountain Lodge*, where you can relax with a spa treatment and stay overnight. *Daily | tel. 64 92 21 00 | cradlemountainlodge.com.au | $$$*

The jungle of Franklin-Gordon Wild Rivers National Park contains many ancient trees

SPORT & ACTIVITIES

CRADLE VALLEY HIKES

Alight from the shuttle at Ronny Creek and stroll along the boardwalk to *Crater Lake* (approx. 1 hr), with a view of Cradle Mountain. Even more imposing is the view from *Marions Lookout* (circular walk 2½ hrs). The route up Cradle Mountain itself is steep, relentless – and worth every step! The final hour-long ascent to the summit involves rock climbing with ropes. For the descent, follow the less-frequented *Horse Track* *(allow 6–8 hrs for the whole route).*

INSIDER TIP
Quiet return journey

OVERLAND TRACK

This trail *(overlandtrack.com.au)* from Cradle Mountain to Lake St Clair is around 65km long. Taking about five days, you will pass through mountainous areas, upland moor, rainforest and deep valleys with spectacular waterfalls. Guided tours are available with *Tasmanian Expeditions (Oct–May | reservations obligatory | from A$2,700 | tasmanianexpeditions.com.au).*

STRAHAN

(G8) **Is this really what the end of the world looks like? The little port of ★ Strahan (pop. 700), with its pretty wooden houses, attracts around 25,000 visitors every year.**

This influx is due in the main to its wildly romantic location among impenetrable bush, and *Macquarie Harbour*, a natural harbour.

EATING & DRINKING

THE STRAHAN VILLAGE

A variety of good accommodation and two restaurants are available right on the harbour. *Daily | The Esplanade | tel. 13 00 06 18 36 | strahanvillage.com.au | $$–$$$*

NIGHTLIFE

INSIDER TIP
Every day is show day

Entertainment with tradition: *The Ship that Never Was* is a witty one-hour play about a successful escape from the penal colony. It's been performed daily since 1984 at 5.30pm in the *Strahan Visitor Centre (ticket A$25).*

AROUND STRAHAN

11 FRANKLIN-GORDON WILD RIVERS NATIONAL PARK ★

Embark on a jouney into the wilderness: the boats of *Gordon River Cruises (from A$135 | 24 Esplanade | tel. 03 64 71 43 00 | gordonrivercruises.com.au)* sail from Macquarie Harbour along the Gordon and through one of the few remaining primeval temperate forests, with trees that are up to 2,000 years old. The tour lasts about six hours and you'll stop along the way at the former penal colony of *Bonnet Island.* G8

12 QUEENSTOWN

40km / 15 mins from Strahan by car

Copper and gold mining transformed this small town (pop. 1,800) into a peculiar lunar landscape. The once-rich copper mine is now closed, and efforts are under way to slowly reforest the landscape. The heritage *West Coast Wilderness Railway (1–6 times a week | from A$45 | wcwr.com.au)* steams along an adventurous route between Queenstown and Strahan. G8

SLEEP WELL IN TASMANIA

PLENTY OF ATMOSPHERE …

It's basic: a narrow bunk, a wooden table and a small window through which some daylight penetrates. But what do you expect if you choose to stay in a cell at the *Maria Island Penitentiary (9 rooms | short.travel/aus66 | $)* on a remote island in the sea that's located off another remote, if larger, island in the sea? And, after hiking through the island's magical but extreme landscapes, you'll be glad of anywhere to rest for the night.

… AND GREAT VIEWS

You'll enjoy a first-class location by the water and top-notch hospitality in the small *Storm Bay B&B (91 White Beach Rd, White Beach | tel. 03 62 69 81 22 | short.travel/aus69 | $$).* Every one of the five guest rooms has either a terrace or a balcony with a view over the bay.

DISCOVERY TOURS

Do you want to get under the skin of the country? Then our discovery tours provide the perfect guide – they include advice on which sights to visit, tips on where to stop for that perfect holiday snap, a choice of the best places to eat and drink, and suggestions for fun activities.

Only accessible at low tide and in good weather: the beach near the Twelve Apostles

DISCOVERY TOURS OVERVIEW

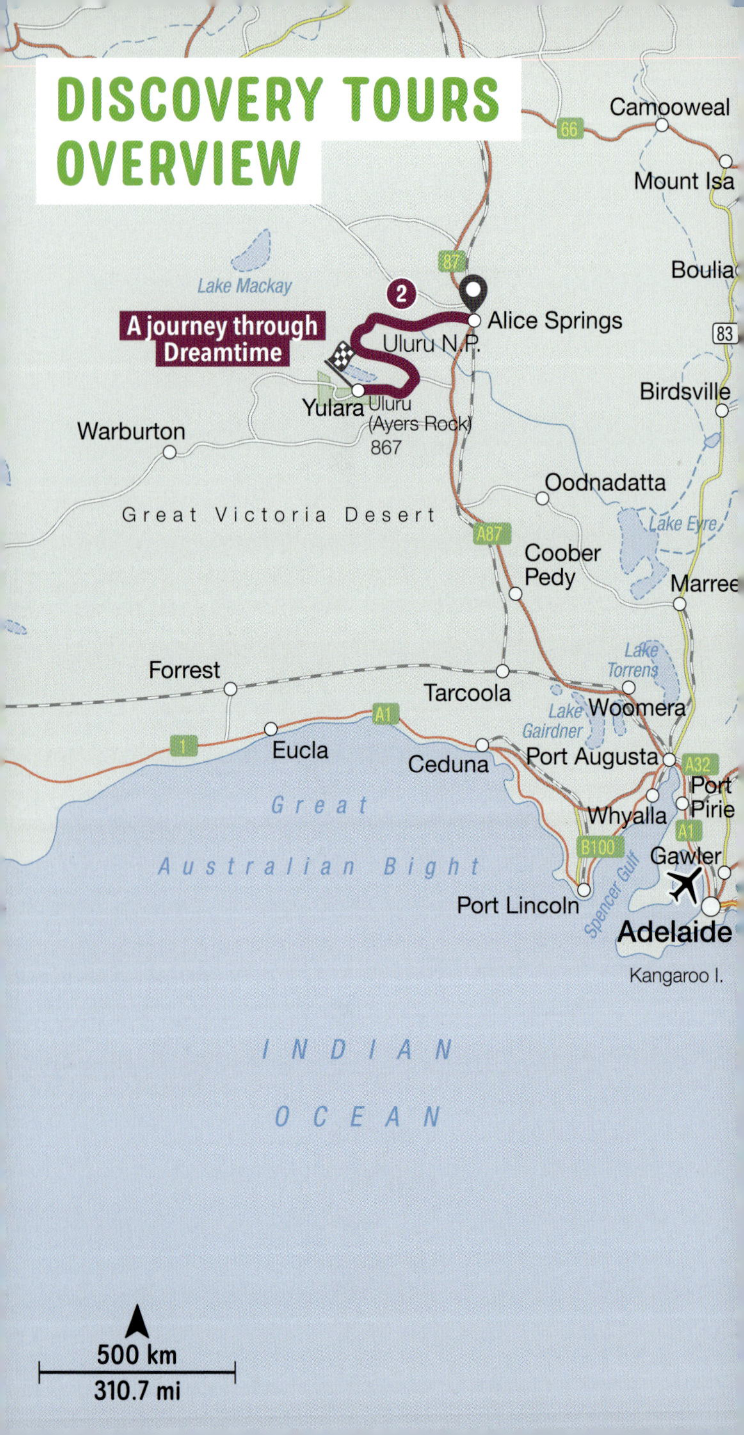

Coral Sea
Great Barrier Reef
Forsayth
Ingham
Townsville
Flinders R.
Bowen
Mackay
Hughenden
Great Dividing Range
Winton
Barcaldine
Emerald
Rockhampton
Gladstone
Longreach
Bundaberg
Fraser Island
Biloela
Windorah
Maryborough
Charleville
Quilpie
Roma
Dalby
Brisbane
Toowoomba
Gold Coast
Rainforest hike in Lamington National Park
Walgett
Bourke
Grafton
Tamworth
Port Macquarie
Wilcannia
Nyngan
Dubbo
New-castle
Maitland
Broken Hill
Darling R.
Sydney
Orange
Tasman Sea
Mildura
Hay
Wollongong
Wagga Wagga
Murray R.
Albury
Canberra
Shepparton
Horsham
Bendigo
Nimmitabel
Melbourne
Cape Howe
Portland
Morwell
Geelong
Spectacular coastal trip: Great Ocean Road
Furneaux Group
Burnie
Smithton
Launceston
Roseberry
Hobart
South East Cape

❶ SPECTACULAR COASTAL TRIP: GREAT OCEAN ROAD ★

- Surf with the pros
- Paddle with platypuses
- Snap a selfie with the Twelve Apostles
- Look a koala in the eye
- Walk to gushing waterfalls in the rainforest
- Learn history through technology at Flagstaff Hill Maritime Village

Melbourne | Flagstaff Hill Maritime Village

4 days | 572km

Driving time: 13 hrs

⑯ **Flagstaff Hill**: book tickets for the show in advance.

DAY 1
❶ Melbourne
72km
❷ Geelong
26 km
❸ Torquay
20km
❹ Anglesea
14km

SURFING HIGHLIGHTS AT BELLS BEACH

Highway M1 takes you from ❶ **Melbourne** ➤ p. 76 to ❷ **Geelong**. Visit the harbour town's **Botanic Gardens** and **art deco seawater pool** on the waterfront, plus the **National Wool Museum** *(daily 10am–5pm | A$12 | 26 Moorabool St | geelongaustralia.com.au/nwm)*.

From Geelong, follow the signs (B100) to ❸ **Torquay**. The settlement is considered the mecca of the surfing scene – as is confirmed by the **Australian National Surfing Museum** *(77 Beach Rd | daily 9am–5pm | A$12 | australiannationalsurfingmuseum.com.au)*. The well-stocked surf shops in town have all the equipment you need, so you can hire a board and emulate the pros who congregate on **Bells Beach** for the international Rip Curl Pro Bells Beach at Easter. A signposted turning at the end of the town goes to the beach. *Back on the Great Ocean Road, drive to your next beach delight: the tiny bathing resort of* ❹ **Anglesea**, where *Harvey Street* has a lookout with fabulous views of the coast. *Another 14km*, and you'll come to

5 Fairhaven Beach, another dreamy beach, and then to 6 Lorne *(lornelink.com.au)*.

The lively tourist centre offers all sorts of food options, surf lessons at Go Ride a Wave *(A$79/2 hrs | goridea wave.com.au)*, and hiking trails to waterfalls, such as Ersking Falls, through the surrounding magnificent rainforest. Now comes one of the loveliest sections of the Great Ocean Road. *It's 49km to* Apollo Bay ➤ p. 84, a charming town with the 7 Marengo Holiday Park *(greatoceanroadparks.com.au/find-a-park/marengo)*, which offers cabins and camping. Learn about the wonders – and the vulnerability – of the local wildlife on a guided tour at the *Wildwife Wonders Sanctuary (admission incl. tour A$59 | wildlifewonders.org.au)*.

5 Fairhaven Beach
16km
6 Lorne
49km
7 Marengo Holiday Park
15km
DAY 2
8 Maits Rest Rainforest Walk
134km
9 Cape Otway Lighthouse

ON THE HUNT FOR PLATYPUSES

Now continue to the densely wooded wilderness of the Great Otway National Park ➤ p. 85. *After only 15km*, a sign on the roadside invites you to the (signposted) 40-minute circular 8 Maits Rest Rainforest Walk. If this puts you in the mood for more, there are many charming hiking routes of varying lengths through the national park that are perfect for observing the animals. Experience platypuses close up on the guided Paddle with the Platypus tour in the late afternoon with Otway Eco Tours *(3–4 hrs | approx. A$85 | tel. 04 19 67 09 85 | platypustours.net.au)*.

Back in the car, *follow the 13km turning to* Cape Otway, which is marked by the white 9 Cape Otway Lighthouse *(daily 9.30am–5pm | A$20 | 3 cabins | tel. 03 52 37 92 40 | lightstation.com | $$$)*, built here on the steep coast by convicts in the middle of the 19th century. You can both visit and spend the night in the historic site.

You can stay in the landmark lighthouse at Cape Otway

DAY 3

76km

⑩ Gibson Steps

2km

⑪ Twelve Apostles Lookout

13km

⑫ Port Campbell

SELFIES WITH THE SANDSTONE APOSTLES

The next stretch of Great Ocean Road is not particularly spectacular – until you get to **Port Campbell National Park** ➤ p. 85 and its **Twelve Apostles**. The first good views of the famous rock formations in the foaming waves are available from the ⑩ **Gibson Steps** to the left of the road. In good weather, you can walk down to the eight remaining limestone stacks from here. *It's about 2km by car to the car park* and the ⑪ **Twelve Apostles Lookout**, from where you can look over the eroded rocks. *You will drive past the* **Loch Ard Gorge** – but make a point of stopping as it's worth it – before reaching the fishing village of ⑫ **Port Campbell**, where you can end the day in one of the lovely restaurants, such as **Waves** *(daily | 29 Lord St | tel. 03 55 98 61 11 | $$).* There are also cafés and a safe bathing beach here. Accommodation is available at the **Southern Ocean Motor Inn** *(southernoceanmotorinn.com | $$).*

DAY 4

WHALES AND DISASTERS

The last section of the panoramic route offers a final look at picturesque coastal formations such as the **London Arch** or **The Grotto**. *At Km13* the road passes the sandy **Bay of Martyrs**, where storm birds nest in the summer, and *20km further on* it merges with the *Princes Highway (A1) towards* **Warrnambool**. Today, this former whaling station attracts whale-watchers, because in the Australian winter (June–September) the southern right whales come here to calve and are easy to observe from the lookout platform on ⑬ **Logans Beach** *(Logans Beach Rd turns off Hopkins Point Rd)*.

72km

⑬ Logans Beach

For lunch, it's worth the drive along *Princes Highway to* ⑭ **Port Fairy** with its listed houses. On the way back, stop off about halfway at the ⑮ **Tower Hill State Game Reserve**, where a fascinating wilderness with countless animals fills the deep crater of an extinct volcano. It is surrounded by a narrow road, where you must always be on the lookout to see wild animals crossing, especially from the late afternoon.

33km

⑭ Port Fairy

17km

⑮ Tower Hill State Game Reserve

Be sure to be back in Warrnambool in the evening, more precisely at the ⑯ **Flagstaff Hill Maritime Village** *(daily 9am–5pm | A$20, show A$33 | Merri St | flagstaffhill.com)*, the reconstruction of a harbour town from the 19th century, for the sound and laser show

16km

⑯ Flagstaff Hill Maritime Village

Magical sights everywhere you look in the grotto near Port Campbell

Tales of the Shipwreck Coast, which brings to life this stretch of coast. For old-fashioned accommodation, look no further than the adjoining, prettily refurbished Lighthouse Lodge *(flagstaffhill.com | $-$$)*.

❷ A JOURNEY THROUGH DREAMTIME

- Drive through the Red Centre in an off-road vehicle
- Picnic at a waterhole
- Scramble around Gosses Bluff Crater
- Watch the sunset at magical Uluru
- Venture to secret gorges and deep pools in the MacDonnell Ranges

Alice Springs — Uluru

3 days — 785km

Driving time: 12 hrs

What to pack: insect protection, road maps, permit. You need a vehicle with four-wheel drive.

Contact the Visitor Information Centre in ❶ **Alice Springs** for information on the current condition of unmade roads and the opening times of the service stations. Fill the car with petrol at the beginning of every day, and be sure to take plenty of drinking water and food with you. Some of the time you will be driving through Aboriginal land. You are not allowed to take alcohol with you. In order to drive the Mereenie Loop Road, you must purchase the *Mereenie Tour Pass ($5)* from the Visitor Information Centre in ❶ **Alice Springs**.

DAY 1

❶ Alice Springs

25km

❷ Simpsons Gap

41km

RED ROCK GORGE

The drive starts in ❶ Alice Springs ➤ p. 119. In the centre, *turn off Stuart Highway onto Larapinta Drive heading west. After 7km*, you'll see the grave site of John Flynn, the founder of Royal Flying Doctor Service ➤ p. 119, on the left side of the road. Take your first break at ❷ Simpsons Gap. It's a short walk through the eucalyptus trees to this waterhole. This place will

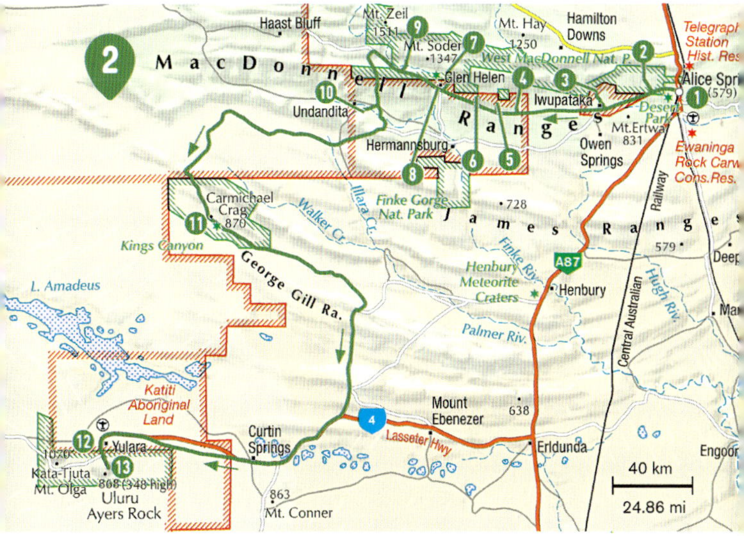

help you to understand why the gorges of the MacDonnell Ranges are of economic as well as cultural importance to local Aboriginal people as they provided them with water and food. *Some 24km further along Larapinta Drive, turn onto* ③ **Standley Chasm**. The chasm is especially spectacular around midday, when the sun turns it into a glowing red corridor.

INSIDER TIP **Lighting up**

Back on Larapinta Drive, you'll leave the road to take Namatjira Drive along the West MacDonnell Ranges. The road ends at ④ **Ellery Creek Big Hole**. The countryside around this large waterhole is extremely varied and very interesting geologically – and perfect for a picnic. Another place on *Namatjira Drive* that is worth stopping at is ⑤ **Serpentine Gorge**. As its name indicates, the gorge winds its way through the rock like a snake.

EARTH HISTORY IN OCHRE

Afterwards, don't ignore the ⑥ **Ochre Pits** as you drive past. They are a cross-section of the 700 million years of this region's geological history. The Western Arrernte people used the pale yellow to rust-red ochre colouring

③ Standley Chasm

60km

④ Ellery Creek Big Hole

16km

⑤ Serpentine Gorge

16km

⑥ Ochre Pits

26km

7 Ormiston Gorge

DAY 2

38km

8 Redbank Gorge

52km

9 Gosses Bluff Crater

182km

for their rock paintings. Pitch your tent at the campsite *(short.travel/aus67)* right by your final stop at **7 Ormiston Gorge**.

CRATER HIKE

Set off before sunrise for the 9.5km Ormiston Pound & Gorge Walk. The gorge, with its "organ pipes", is definitely worth a visit. *Namatjira Drive* is now a dirt track, and will take you through the fresh morning air to idyllic **8 Redbank Gorge**, before you *change direction to the southwest* and the Tnorala Conservation Reserve with the **9 Gosses Bluff Crater**, which is the result of a meteorite impact about 140 million years ago and is worshipped by the Western Arrernte people as a holy site. If the very bumpy *10km gravel road* doesn't bother you, you'll finally reach a dead end in the vast crater (5km diameter). The silence when you turn off the engine is unbelievable. A *signposted hiking path* takes you even closer to the crater.

You still have about 180km of gravel road to travel to reach Watarrka National Park and ⑩ **Kings Canyon** ➤ p. 121. *At the next junction, turn right onto Mereenie Loop Road (permit required)*, and from now on you'll be travelling across Aboriginal land. The best options for accommodation, including a campsite and views of an amazing starry sky, are available at the **Kings Canyon Resort**.

⑩ Kings Canyon

ULURU AT DUSK

DAY 3

307km

⑪ Ayers Rock Resort (Yulara)

22km

⑫ Uluru

An approximately two- to three-hour walk will take you through the canyon in the morning and to the made-up route *along Luritja Road, where you turn right onto Lasseter Highway* to Uluru. Plan the day so that upon arrival at the ⑪ **Ayers Rock Resort (Yulara)** ➤ p. 122 you have enough time to check in or ptich your tent and take up your position near ⑫ **Uluru** ➤ p. 121 before sunset (*sunset times: short.travel/aus1*) and the **Winjiri Wiru light show**.

700 million years of Earth's history at the Ochre Pits

❸ RAINFOREST HIKE IN LAMINGTON NATIONAL PARK

- Discover the jungle on well-marked paths
- Find one waterfall after another
- Take a break between the eucalyptus trees
- Gaze out over the rainforest
- Wade through a river in your hiking boots

Car park, Binna Burra	Car park, Binna Burra
7–8 hrs	16km
Walking time: 5½ hrs	Height: 680m
Difficulty: easy	

What to pack: insect protection, drinking water (at least 1.5 litres/person), hiking map.

Up-to-date information on the accessibility of the trail is available from the ranger (*Mon–Fri 1.30–3.30pm, Sat/Sun 9am–5pm | tel. 07 55 33 35 84*) or at *short.travel/aus2*.

To get to the ❶ **car park** in Binna Burra, follow Binna Burra Road to its end.

❶ Binna Burra car park

5km

❷ Coomera Falls Lookout

100m

FROM WATERFALL TO WATERFALL …

You start at the top: the ❶ **car park** in Binna Burra is already at an altitude of 800m. *First of all, follow the Border Track*. The well-constructed track is basically the main artery in the dense network of hiking trails in the national park. Behind towering evergreen brush box trees *turn onto the Coomera Falls Circuit and enjoy a gentle stroll down*.

The route becomes steeper towards the ❷ **Coomera Falls Lookout**, where you will have impressive waterfall views right in front of you – and your camera lens. Time for a break! Coomera River plunges 64m, while the nearby **Yarrabilgong Falls** drop an impressive

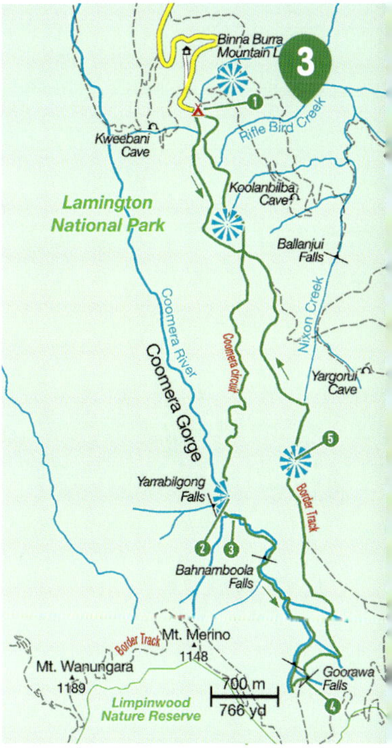

160m. In view of the sparkling surroundings, it's hardly surprising that the air is so wonderfully fresh. But be careful if it rains: it's easy to lose your footing on the slippery ground!

You'll soon leave the thicket behind you on the ascending path, and arrive at a lighter eucalyptus forest. Allow yourself a rest on the edge of the 160m-deep ❸ **Coomera River Gorge** and let the spectacular surroundings work their magic on you.

... AND BANK TO BANK

You'll soon cross the Coomera River for the first time. Keep your hiking boots on because of the leeches, even though insect repellent is supposed to keep these harmless but tiresome bloodsuckers at bay. *You'll change banks a number of times over the next 3.5km*, past the **Bahnamboola Falls**, **Gwongarragong Falls** and **Chigigunya Falls**, to name but a few of the now-frequent waterfalls. The blue Lamington spiny crayfish is at home in the numerous water-filled rock pools.

By the time you get to the ❹ **Goorawa Falls**, *where the path rejoins the Border Track*, you'll have managed more than half of the route – and will have earned yourself another stop (for lunch). *From now on, follow the route to the north – and uphill: you have about 100m to climb.*

At the top, Antarctic beech forest is a key feature of the vegetation: a woodland that only survives in cooler climates on this continent. In clear weather, there are wonderful views over the gorges of the high plateau, e.g. from ❺ **Joahla Lookout**, before the Border Track takes you back to the ❶ **car park** in Binna Burra.

❸ Coomera River Gorge

3.5km

❹ Goorawa Falls

3km

❺ Joahla Lookout

4.5km

❶ Binna Burra car park

GOOD TO KNOW

HOLIDAY BASICS

ARRIVAL

GETTING THERE

Flights from London to the east coast of Australia take 23+ hours. The long journey is more pleasant if you stop over in Singapore or Hong Kong (from London approx. 15 hours, on to Sydney eight hours), for example. Depending on the time of year, an economy class return ticket from London can cost anything from around £900 upwards. Cathay Pacific also offers a comfortable and attractively priced premium economy class. Direct flights from the west coast of the USA to Sydney take about 15 hours, with ticket prices starting at US$860 return. Don't forget, when comparing prices, to check whether taxes and other fees are included. Some airlines such as Qantas *(qantas.com.au)* and Cathay Pacific *(cathaypacific.com/en)* offer cheap or free tickets for domestic flights within Australia when you purchase an international ticket.

OFFSET YOUR FLIGHT

The return flight is likely to be the most environmentally damaging part of your holiday. A single traveller on a return flight from London to Sydney generates 8.9 tonnes of CO_2. You can offset this emission at *co2.myclimate.org/en/flight_calculators/new* (and other organisations) for around £212. The money is used to fund climate protection projects around the world.

GETTING IN

To enter Australia you'll need a free tourist visa that can usually be issued

An Instagram moment on the Stuart Highway, which links north and south

or applied for when purchasing a plane ticket (eVisitor visa). It is valid for a stay of up to three months. It is strictly forbidden to take paid employment of any kind and failing to observe this law could result in a heavy fine. People between 18 and 30 years of age may apply for a Working Holiday visa valid for up to 12 months, which allows them to accept temporary employment *(immi.homeaffairs.gov.au/visas)*. Information: *Australian High Commission | Strand, London WC2B 4LA | tel. 020 7379 4334 | uk.embassy.gov.au)*.

Time difference: +8 / +9½ / +10 hrs

There are three time zones in Australia:
Western Australia: Western Standard Time (GMT +8 hours)
Northern Territory and South Australia: Central Standard Time (GMT +9.5 hours)
Other states: Eastern Standard Time (GMT +10 hours).
Daylight Saving time in most states (except Queensland, Northern Territory and Western Australia) is between the first Sunday in October and the first Sunday in April.

CLIMATE & WHEN TO GO

The southeast (New South Wales, Tasmania, Victoria and South Australia), as well as Western Australia south of the Tropic of Capricorn, are best visited between October and April (spring and summer). Queensland, Northern Territory and the north of Western Australia are best visited between April and November (the dry season). At other times of the year it is generally cool in the south, and hot and

Adapter Type I

The mains voltage is 240 volt AC. Most standard European devices operate without any problem but you do need an adapter, available for example at airports, luggage shops or chemists. Visitors from Canada and the US may need a voltage converter.

sticky in the north (north of the Tropic of Capricorn) – and it can rain very heavily. For current weather information go to bom.gov.au.

Accommodation, and campsites in particular, are often fully booked during the summer holidays in December and January and over long weekends. What's more, prices can double or even triple at these times.

GETTING AROUND

CAR HIRE

If you want to see more than the standard tourist highlights along the coasts, it's a good idea to hire a car. Small cars are often cheaper to hire than in Europe (from approx. A$40/day without insurance), and diesel and petrol are also cheaper (approx. A$1.80/litre). For a price comparison go to *vroomvroomvroom.com.au.*

If you want to save money or like being outdoors, book a camper van (from approx. A$65/day without insurance). Whether you need a four-wheel-drive or not obviously depends on the route you're planning. Make sure your car hire company permits off-road driving (on unsurfaced/gravel roads) and take out a fully comprehensive insurance policy without co-payment. Be careful about supplements, for example if you plan to drop the car in a different city, or extra charges for credit card payments. An international driving licence is obligatory for some companies. The best offers for campervans can be found online. Major hire companies include *Maui (maui.com.au)* and *Apollo (apollocamper.com).*

Australians drive on the left and give way to traffic coming from the right. In general, the speed limit in a built-up area is 50kmh and 100kmh in rural areas. True motorways can only be found near major cities. Many highways are in fact single-lane country roads with occasional overtaking lanes.

INTERCITY BUSES

With the exception of the East Coast, Australia's bus and rail network is quite sparse. It is often a good idea to buy bus passes for intercity journeys before starting your journey. Such passes either allow you to make an unlimited number of stops on any chosen route, are divided into categories according to distance, or give you a reduction of 50 per cent. The market is dominated by *Greyhound (greyhound.com.au).*

INTERCITY TRAINS

The absolute best way to grasp the scale of this simply enormous country is on the intercity *Indian Pacific (sleeper cabins from A$3,690)*, which runs from Sydney via Adelaide and the Nullarbor Plain to Perth. The whole trip takes three days, departing from Sydney on Wednesdays and Perth on Saturdays. Other intercity trains run from Adelaide through the Red Centre to Darwin *(The Ghan)* and between Melbourne and Adelaide *(The Overland)*. Limited seats mean train trips should be organised as early as possible. Information and booking: *Great Southern Rail (tel. 08 82 13 44 01 | greatsouthernrail.com.au)*.

INTERNAL FLIGHTS

Competition among budget airlines is huge: try *Jetstar (jetstar.com)* and *Virgin Australia (virginaustralia.com)*. Prices for inland flights vary considerably. The earlier you book, the better for your budget. *Regional Express (rex.com.au)* also flies to remote regions.

EMERGENCIES

EMERGENCY CALLS

Emergencies (tel. 000). Callers must then specify which service they require: fire, police or ambulance.

CONSULATES & EMBASSIES

BRITISH HIGH COMMISSION

130 Commonwealth Av, Canberra, Yarralumla ACT 2600 | tel. 262 70 66 66 | gov.uk/world/organisations/british-high-commission-canberra

Apart from the High Commission, the United Kingdom has nine other offices in Australia, including the British Consulate-General in Sydney.

BRITISH CONSULATE-GENERAL

Level 16, Gateway Building, 1 Macquarie Place, Sydney, NSW 2000 | tel. +61 2 82 47 22 00 | gov.uk/world/organisations/british-consulate-general-sydney

EMBASSY OF THE UNITED STATES OF AMERICA

Moonah Place, Canberra, Yarralumla ACT 2600 | tel. +61 2 62 14 56 00 | au.usembassy.gov

EMBASSY OF IRELAND

20 Arkana St, Canberra, Yarralumla ACT 2600 | tel. +61 2 62 14 00 00 | ireland.ie/en/australia/canberra

HEALTH

UK and Irish citizens, and those from several other European nations, are entitled to free reciprocal Medicare treatment in Australian hospitals and at GPs, although there are certain restrictions. It is best to familiarise yourself beforehand with the conditions of the reciprocal arrangement as it does not, for example, cover private hospitals, which can be very expensive. It is always worth taking out additional health insurance before your journey. Most hospitals offer an interpreting service for patients who don't have fluent English.

ESSENTIALS

ACCOMMODATION/CAMPING

Hotels in major cities are expensive *(A$115–290 for 3- to 4-star hotels)*; flats/apartments are often a better alternative: they are bigger, better equipped and slightly cheaper. There is also a good choice of holiday homes for rent *(stayz.com.au)*. Outside urban centres there are numerous motels *(A$90–150)*. Campsites *(campermate.com | campsaustraliawide.com, also lists free sites)* often have cabins and motel rooms *(A$70–140)*. B&B is also popular *(bedandbreakfast.com.au)*, as is a stay on a station, as farms in Australia are called *(farmstayaustralia.com.au)*. Good accommodation can be found at short notice at *wotif.com.au* and *ozbargain.com.au*. Youth hostels and backpacker hostels – of which there are many – also have cheap double rooms. Rooms or even houses available privately can be found under *airbnb.com.au*, *homestayweb.com* and *couchsurfing.org*.

ALCOHOL

You have to be 18 to consume alcohol. Many towns and cities have designated dry zones – parks and beach sections where no alcohol may be consumed. It is strictly forbidden to take alcohol into Aboriginal territories even if asked to do so.

BANK HOLIDAYS & FESTIVALS

1 Jan	New Year
26 Jan	Australia Day/Survival Day
March/April	Good Friday & Easter Monday
25 April	Anzac Day
1st Tues in Nov	Melbourne Cup Day
14 Nov	King's birthday
25/26 Dec	Christmas

BRING YOUR OWN

Bring your own or *BYO* on the front door of a restaurant means they don't serve wine – instead you get to bring your own. Buy it in the nearest *bottleshop*, often attached to pubs. The restaurant opens and refrigerates the bottles and charges a small fee, *corkage (from approx. A$10/bottle)*.

CURRENCY

The unit of currency is the Australian dollar (A$). There are 5, 10, 20, 50 and 100 Australian dollar notes; 1 and 2 dollar coins; and 5, 10, 20 and 50 cent coins. Prices for goods and services are comparable to those in Britain. Some food is slightly more expensive. For the current exchange rate, see *xe.com*.

CUSTOMS

It is forbidden to import fruit, vegetables or meat into Australia due to the risk of disease. You may bring in 50 cigarettes or 25g of tobacco and 2.25 litres of alcohol per person duty-free, as well as personal items and gifts up to a value of A$900.

For purchases of more than A$300 in a shop in Australia you can reclaim the 10 per cent VAT at the airport when you depart. You must show the bill and items purchased at customs.

INTERNET & WIFI

Australia has good internet connections, especially in towns and cities. Almost every pub offers free WiFi, as do most guesthouses and hotels.

INSIDER TIP
Free internet

There are also plenty of hotspots in the towns and cities *(short.travel/aus31)* where you can access the internet free of charge. The local libraries offer internet access, and often computers as well, for you to use for a specific length of time.

MONEY

Money can be changed, cash obtained from ATMs with bank and credit cards, and even traveller's cheques can be cashed without any problem at banks in major cities and tourist centres *(opening times generally Mon–Fri 9am–4pm)*. Credit cards (especially Visa and MasterCard) are widely accepted. That said, it's still worth having cash in the outback.

HOW MUCH DOES IT COST?

Coffee	*£3.10 for a cappuccino*
Beer	*£4.85 for a pint in a pub*
Fast food	*£5.30 for a meal and soft drink*
Petrol	*£0.90 for a litre of regular*
Cinema	*£10.60 for a ticket*
Surfboard	*£14.15 for 2 hrs' rental*

OPENING HOURS

Restaurants, pubs, food shops and information offices in the larger towns are generally open every day. In cities, supermarkets are usually open from around 7am to 10pm, sometimes with shorter hours at weekends. Shops in shopping centres usually open from 9am to 5pm and until 8 or 9pm on Thursdays. However, in the country, shops and restaurants are often closed over the weekend. And in the outback, some service stations, motels and small restaurants often close in the early evening.

POST

A postcard or a letter to Europe costs A$3 and takes about two weeks to arrive. Further information: *auspost.com.au*

PHONE & MOBILE PHONES

The international dialling code for Australia is 61, followed by the area code without the 0, e.g. 2 for Sydney (02). From Australia, the dialling code is 00 11 +44 for the UK, 00 11 +1 for the USA and Canada. Toll-free numbers start with 1800; six-digit numbers that start with 1300 are charged as local calls.

Prepaid cards for mobile phones for use in Australia can be bought before your journey for a set fee that normally includes a number of free calls and data for a set period. If you are staying longer in Australia, it's best to get an Australian sim card, e.g. from Optus, Vodafone or Telstra. The best network in Australia is *Telstra (telstra.com.au)*. Satellite telephones are an alternative for use in the outback. These can also be rented, with prepaid credit *(e.g. rentasatphone.com.au)*.

SMOKING

Smoking in, and in the vicinity of, all outdoor eating areas is not allowed. Many beaches and most pedestrian zones are also non-smoking. Violations are punished with high fines.

TOURIST INFORMATION

Tourism Australia *(australia.com)*; Tourism New South Wales *(visit nsw.com)*; Tourism Queensland *(queensland.com)*; Tourism Northern Territory *(tourismandeventsnt.com.au)*; Tourism Western Australia *(western australia.com)*; Tourism South Australia *(southaustralia.com)*; Tourism Tasmania *(tourismtasmania.com.au)*.

WEATHER IN SYDNEY

High season
Low season

	JAN	FEB	MARCH	APRIL	MAY	JUNE	JULY	AUG	SEPT	OCT	NOV	DEC
Daytime temperature	26°	26°	24°	22°	19°	16°	16°	17°	19°	22°	23°	25°
Night-time temperature	18°	18°	17°	14°	11°	9°	8°	9°	11°	13°	16°	17°
Hours of sunshine per day	7	7	6	5	5	4	5	6	6	7	7	7
Rainy days per month	7	8	8	7	5	9	5	7	7	9	8	8
Sea temperature in °C	23	24	23	20	18	18	16	17	18	19	19	21

Hours of sunshine per day · Rainy days per month · Sea temperature in °C

Aerial view of Sydney's Royal Botanic Gardens

HOLIDAY VIBES

FOR RELAXATION & CHILLING

FOR BOOKWORMS & FILM BUFFS

DOWN UNDER

As usual you're guaranteed to laugh out loud while reading American journalist Bill Bryson's travel experiences in Australia (2001).

TRACKS

Back in the late 1970s, Australian Robyn Davidson flew to world fame when she set out alone with a dog and four camels on the 2,700km journey from Alice Springs to the West Coast (1980).

RABBIT-PROOF FENCE

A moving insight into the tragic story of the Stolen Generation: forcibly separated from their parents, three girls dare to escape from the "Native Settlement" and make the long, uncertain journey home (2002).

THE CASTLE

The Australian classic. It might not offer action-packed plot twists, but this film keeps its audience spellbound throughout and, above all, makes them laugh (1997).

PLAYLIST ON THE ROAD AGAIN

0:58

COLD CHISEL – KHE SANH
One of the most Australian songs of all time.

INXS – NEVER TEAR US APART
Australian rock legend Michael Hutchence and band still make our playlist.

POWDERFINGER – SUNSET
The soundtrack for a road trip along the Australian coast.

MIDNIGHT OIL – DIESEL AND DUST (ALBUM)
Peter Garrett was not just a minister, but a singer too.

KYLIE MINOGUE – COME INTO MY WORLD
One of many global hits by Australia's pop princess.

YOTHU YINDI – TREATY
This band mixes Aboriginal music traditions with rock band sounds

The holiday soundtrack is available on **Spotify** under **MARCO POLO** Australia

Or scan this code with the Spotify app

ONLINE

ABORIGINAL VISIT
diversetravel.com.au provides tours that give an excellent insight into Aboriginal Australian cultures.

EAT LIKE A KING
agfg.com.au is up to date with the best restaurants and cafés.

TRAVEL REPORTS
"Seventy best Australian travel blogs and websites": blog.feedspot.com/australia_travel_blog.

KIP IN THE OUTBACK
Where better to experience the outback than on a remote farm or in a secret caravan park? *outbackbeds.com.au* lists unique spots to stay overnight.

WHAT'S THE WEATHER LIKE?
Reliable source for weather forecasts and weather warnings, including rain radar: *bom.gov.au*.

INDEX

WE WANT TO HEAR FROM YOU!

Did you have a great holiday? Is there something on your mind? Whatever it is, let us know! Whether you want to praise the guide, alert us to errors or give us a personal tip – MARCO POLO would be pleased to hear from you.

We do everything we can to provide the very latest information for your trip. Nevertheless, despite all of our authors' thorough research, errors can creep in. MARCO POLO does not accept any liability for this.

Please contact us by email: **sales@heartwoodpublishing.co.uk**

PICTURE CREDITS
Cover photo: Uluru (Huber-images: J. Huber)
Photos: DUMONT Bildarchiv: T. Babovic (30, 192/193), C. Emmler (10, 140/141, 163), T. Widmann (117); HUBER IMAGES: St. Cellai (123), J. Cliffe (80/81), G. Cozzi (137), B. Mitchell (60, 115), M. Rellini (48, 170/171), TC (83, Huber-images: TC (26/27); laif: C. Emmler (12), Ch. Heeb (168), G. Theis (184/185); laif/hemis.fr (121); laif/Loop Images: A. Hare (51); laif/robertharding: R. Harding Production (32/33), P.-A. Hoffmann (6/7), M. Runkel (44/45); lookphotos: D. Fuchs (153, 155), P.-A. Hoffmann (8/9), H. Leue (65); mauritius images: W. Bibikow (13), I. Boelter (156/157), cgimanufaktur (88/89), R. Linkel (2/3), I. Oeland (94, 167); mauritius images/AGF/Bildagentur RM (118); mauritius images/Alamy (25, 131), A. Bain (138/139), G. Belfour Evans (180/181), R. Ben-Ari (98), M. Berry (47), D. Chrastek (86/87), Imagevixen (124/125), Lkonya (177), G. Marshall (34/35), H. Maunder (106), A. McComiskey (52), S. Nerrie (149), I. Oeland (56/57), S. Reboredo (33), W. Robinson (68), J. Russell (66), E. Schlogl (135), P. Scholey (78), A. Scott (164), T. Vyshnya (40/41), D. Wall (113), T. Whitefoot (100); mauritius images/Alamy/Danita Delimont (160); mauritius images/blickwinkel: B. Leitner (108/109); mauritius images/Cavan Images (132), A. Peacock (front cover flap, inside front cover, 1); mauritius images/Cultura (28/29); mauritius images/foodcollection (29); mauritius images/fStop: T. Titz (21); mauritius images/imageBROKER: K. Petersen (175), N. Probst (36/37), M. Weber (102); mauritius images/John Warburton-Lee (97); mauritius images/Loop Images: A. Hare (53); mauritius images/Radius Images (84); mauritius images/robertharding: F. Fell (11), M. Simoni (63); mauritius images/Westend61 (inside back cover); mauritius images/Westend61/Fotofeeling (72/73); C. Melville (195); Shutterstock.com: idiz (14/15), R. Balasko (16/17), J. Carnemolla (22), J. Makulewicz (105), A. Manciagli (70), myphotobank.com.au (142/143); T.P. Widmann (151), Olga Kashubin (191)

4th Edition – fully revised and updated 2026
Worldwide Distribution: Heartwood Publishing Ltd, Bath, United Kingdom www.heartwoodpublishing.co.uk

Authors: Esther Blank, Bruni Gebauer, Stefan Huy, Corinna Melville, Urs Wälterlin
Editor: Jens Bey **Picture editor:** Barbara Mehrl
Cartography: © KOMPASS-Karten GmbH, A-6020 Innsbruck/MAIRDUMONT, D-73760 Ostfildern (pp. 38–39, 172–173, 176, 179, 183, back cover, pull-out map); © KOMPASS-Karten GmbH, kompass.de under licence from © OpenStreetMap Contributors, osm.org/copyright (pp. 42–43, 54, 58–59, 74–75, 77, 90–91, 93, 110–111, 126–127, 129, 144–145, 146, 158–159)
Cover design and pull-out map cover design: Eggers+Diaper, Aachent
Page design: Langenstein Communication GmbH, Ludwigsburg

Heartwood Publishing credits:
Translated from the German by Sophie Blacksell Jones, Madeleine Taylor-Laidler, Christopher Wynne and Mo Croasdale
Editors: Kate Michell, Sophie Blacksell Jones, Rosamund Sales
Prepress: Summerlane Books, Bath
Printed in India

GPSR Compliance: MairDumont GmbH, Marco-Polo-Str, 73760 Ostfildern, Deutschland.
Email: info@marcopolo.de

MARCO POLO AUTHOR
CORINNA MELVILLE
Corinna's internship at an Australian newspaper wasn't quite what she expected: instead of egg-laying mammals and deserted islands, she found herself reporting on rather more European events. Nonetheless, her year abroad turned into a lifelong love for the country, which she has called home since 2008. She now lives with her family in Adelaide.